REJECTION

Keeping You In

and

Others Out

HENRY W. WRIGHT

4178 Crest Highway
Thomaston, Georgia 30286

www.beinhealth.com

Copyright Notice

Disclaimer

This ministry does not seek to be in conflict with any medical or psychiatric practices nor do we seek to be in conflict with any church and its religious doctrines, beliefs or practices. We are not a part of medicine or psychology, yet we work to make them more effective, rather than working against them. We believe many human problems are fundamentally spiritual with associated physiological and psychological manifestations. This information is intended for your general knowledge only. Information is presented only to give insight into disease, its problems and its possible solutions in the area of disease eradication and/or prevention. It is not a substitute for medical advice or treatment for specific medical conditions or disorders. You should seek prompt medical care for any specific health issues. Treatment modalities around your specific health issues are between you and your physician.

As pastors, ministers, and individuals of this ministry, we are not responsible for a person's disease, nor are we responsible for his/her healing. All we can do is share what we see about a problem. We are not professionals; we are not healers. We are only ministers administering the Scriptures, and what they say about this subject, along with what the medical and scientific communities have also observed in line with this insight. There is no guarantee that any person will be healed or any disease be prevented. The fruits of this teaching will come forth out of the relationship between the person and God based on these insights given and applied. This ministry is patterned after the following scriptures: 2 Corinthians 5:18-20; 1 Corinthians 12; Ephesians 4; Mark 16:15-20.

Preface

This booklet was developed from a teaching to a live audience and has been kept in a conversational format. It is designed to reach a personal level with the reader rather than present a structured, theological presentation. Many times the reader will feel that Pastor Henry is talking directly to him/her. The frequent use of the pronoun "you" is meant to penetrate the human heart for conviction, not for accusation.

...wherein he hath made us accepted in the beloved.

Ephesians 1:6

Table of Contents

REJECTION

Introduction

[9]There remaineth therefore a rest to the people of God.
[10]For he that is entered into his rest, he also hath ceased from his own works, as God did from his.
[11]Let us labour therefore to enter into that rest, lest any man fall after the same example of unbelief.   Hebrews 4:9-11

Rejection is a form of unbelief. It is as dangerous as unbelief itself. It is as dangerous as faithlessness. Rejection is a form of unbelief because Rejection **says that you are not accepted of God, and in order to be accepted of God you have to be accepted of men first. It sets man as your god** by declaring that who you are and who you are not rests on a human who accepts you or does not accept you. That makes God a liar.

> **There are no other beings
> greater than God.
> They do not exist.**

If you make man your god and also whether someone accepts you or not as the basis of your righteousness and your acceptance by God, then you are in idolatry — self-idolatry and idolatry of men. Idolatry is the first of the Ten Commandments that brings a curse to the third and fourth generation (Exodus 20:5).

You are not from men. You may say you are because you had a mother and father. In Psalm 139, David said you come from God. He said that before you became a fetus within the womb, even before you were ever conceived, God knew your parts. He knew whether you would have blue eyes, or brown eyes, or whatever your characteristics are. God knew every bit of who you would be long before you or your parents were conceived, before your grandparents were conceived, and before Adam and Eve were conceived. He knew you from the foundation of the world, and you were neither an accident nor mistake. You are known of God and accepted of God through Jesus Christ, and you have to accept that. You have to accept that you are no accident because if you say you are an accident, then you make God a liar.

You cannot defeat Rejection
unless you have dealt with
Bitterness
and
Envy and Jealousy.

Prerequisite for Victory

You cannot defeat Rejection unless you have dealt with Bitterness and Envy and Jealousy in your life. It is impossible because you do not have any tools to work with. You may want to be free of Rejection, but if you do not have Bitterness, Envy and Jealousy settled in your life spiritually, you will never stand in your freedom from Rejection. It is impossible. It is quite a paradox. Rejection is a *doorway* for Bitterness and Envy and Jealousy, but you cannot defeat

Rejection until you have defeated Bitterness and Envy and Jealousy.

Hebrews 4 talks about a place of rest. Not having Bitterness within you is a place of rest. Not having Envy or Jealousy is a place of rest. Not having any feelings of Rejection is a place of rest.

Hebrews 4:11 says, "Let us labor therefore to enter into that rest" of freedom from Bitterness, freedom from Envy and Jealousy, and freedom from Rejection. That is the rest that God has purposed for you from the foundation of the world. Unbelief will keep you from going into that rest.

> **For the word of God is quick, and powerful, and sharper than any two-edged sword, piercing even to the dividing asunder of soul and spirit, and of the joints and marrow, and is a discerner of the thoughts and intents of the heart.**
>
> Hebrews 4:12

It says, "thoughts and intents of the heart." That does not mean soul; it means spirit. As a man thinks in his heart, so is he (Proverbs 23:7).

A Mixture

Who you are could be a mixture of two kingdoms, spiritually. If you were not a mixture, you would not need to be sanctified. Even though it was a finished product at the cross, when you became born again it was not a finished product in your personal life. What Christ did is a completed work. Now **it is something you have to appropriate to your life in your generation.** He made it possible.

If Christ had not finished it at the cross, it would not be possible for you to be free of anything because He would not have defeated it. Because He has defeated it does not mean that you do not have to appropriate it. Half of the church is running around today claiming they are free without appropriation and yet wondering why they are insane and have diseases. They are confessing the freedom without the appropriation. **Promise without discernment is still bondage.**

Who are you? You are a little bit of a mixture of heaven, and you are a little bit of a mixture of hell. It is like a scale balancing from day to day. Which is the greater power in your life? You know what you are struggling with. You know what you are dealing with. The Bible says a man knows the thoughts of his own heart.

> **For what man knoweth the things of a man, save the spirit of man which is in him? even so the things of God knoweth no man, but the Spirit of God.**   1 Corinthians 2:11

God knows the thoughts of a man's heart because the Word of God is a discerner of the thoughts and intents of the heart (Hebrews 4:12). Jesus is the Word of God. If He knows the number of the hairs of your head (Matthew 10:30), of course He knows your thoughts.

The devil does not know your thoughts because he is not omniscient. He is a created being himself. He does not have the faculties of omniscience. He does not have the faculties of being omnipresent. He does not have the faculties of being omnipotent. He does not have the faculties of being omnificent. He is a created being, but the devil can project thoughts into you. God the Holy Spirit can also project thoughts into you.

Do you know how the devil knows your thoughts? He will give you a thought and then you do it. He knows it is exactly what he put in your mind. You think he is reading your mind. No, he gave you the thought, you acted on it, and he sat back to see if you listened. You did listen. You meditated on it, you went into motion, and you did it.

He whispers, "Yes, that is your thought." Then you blame the devil for something that he did just a little bit differently than what you think. He gave you the thoughts and you acted on them.

The Bible says in 1 John that whosoever is born of God cannot sin, but whosoever sinneth is of the devil.

> **⁸He that committeth sin is of the devil; for the devil sinneth from the beginning. For this purpose the Son of God was manifested, that he might destroy the works of the devil.**
> **⁹Whosoever is born of God doth not commit sin; for his seed remaineth in him: and he cannot sin, because he is born of God.** 1 John 3:8-9

Rejection is sin. Envy and Jealousy is sin. Bitterness is sin. It is as much sin as murder, homosexuality, strife, adultery, or fornication.

James 2:10 says that if you offend in one point of the law, you are guilty of all the law. If you went ahead and said, "Well, this is a sin that God likes, and this is a sin that God does not like. I go to church, I keep the Sabbath, I pay my tithe, I give to the poor, and I do all these good things." But if you have unforgiveness in your heart, it is as much a sin as adultery.

When you look in Romans 1, Galatians 5 and Mark 7 at the definition of sin, you will find that strife and murder are in the same chapter, in the same verse. Adultery and strife are found together as equals, as copartners.

²⁹Being filled with all unrighteousness, fornication, wickedness, covetousness, maliciousness; full of envy, murder, debate, deceit, malignity; whisperers,
³⁰Backbiters, haters of God, despiteful, proud, boasters, inventors of evil things, disobedient to parents,   Romans 1:29-30

²⁰Idolatry, witchcraft, hatred, variance, emulations, wrath, strife, seditions, heresies,
²¹Envyings, murders, drunkenness, revellings, and such like: of the which I tell you before, as I have also told you in time past, that they which do such things shall not inherit the kingdom of God.   Galatians 5:20-21

²¹For from within, out of the heart of men, proceed evil thoughts, adulteries, fornications, murders,
²²Thefts, covetousness, wickedness, deceit, lasciviousness, an evil eye, blasphemy, pride, foolishness:
²³All these evil things come from within, and defile the man.   Mark 7:21-23

The Word of God is quick and powerful and is a discerner of the thoughts and intents of the heart. There is a difference between a thought and an intent. You cannot have intent without a thought, but you can have the thought and not have the intent. Intent is the thought set into motion. You can have unforgiveness in your heart as a thought, but you cast it down as an imagination and it does not go into motion. **Temptation is not sin.** You can have every evil thought known to man and if you do not have the intent behind it and put it into motion, it is not sin to you. It is just temptation.

Maybe Rejection has become so much a part of your life and nature that you would not know what to do without it. It is going to be scary for you to exist without Rejection being part of your thinking. You are spending 80% of your time preparing to be rejected and then convincing yourself that you are. If that is not good enough, you go ahead and create a scene somewhere to make sure you are rejected.

An Evil Spirit

Rejection is an evil spirit. It is not an emotion, it is not a concept, it is not a philosophy, and it is not an ideology. **Rejection is a living being – an invisible, disembodied entity.** Its name is Rejection and it manifests by its nature wanting to become part of your nature so the two of you can be one together. It needs you. You are the medium and it is the spokesman. It is the parasite and you are the carrier. To Rejection, you are a medium of existence in the physical world and a medium of conversation.

It needs you because it must manifest by its nature. I have seen so many people who get convicted because of an evil spirit in their life. They try to suppress it and they try to act like it is not there. Then they go through all these mechanisms of religion trying to surround it and deal with it, and stand on it, and sit on it, and all kinds of things. But I have learned one thing about an evil spirit: **it has no choice but to manifest its nature.** When it is not manifesting, it is in torment and you are in peace. When it is manifesting, you are in torment and it is in peace. Evil spirits are driven to manifest. They continually seek a physical body to manifest through. It has no other vehicle of expression.

That is why we read in Hebrews 4:12, "The Word of God comes, quick and powerful, is able to separate the soul from the spirit, and is a discerner of the thoughts and intents of the heart." The Word of God discerns your invisible thinking. In 1 Corinthians 12, one of the nine gifts of the Holy Spirit is discerning of spirits. It is a shocking thing to find out that **thoughts within your very spirit and mind are not you** and yet you act out things that are not you. Talk about being a puppet! You say, "O God, I do not want to be a clone. God is not going to put me in a box. I'm not going to be a dummy hanging on a string. God isn't going to make me do it." You already are a puppet. You are dangling. They have you and all you do is go around every day and act out their nature and cohabit and participate with them. Then you wonder why you are all goofed up, why you do not feel good, why you are in depression and why your body is reacting.

The foundation for freedom is defeating Bitterness, Envy and Jealousy, and Rejection. They have to be brought under control at all cost in your life, because if you do not, you are just going to be a tale that is told.

Your battle is in relationship with God, yourself and others. That is the foundation for disease and that has to be resolved before healing can come. You must resolve your relationship with God. You must accept yourself and who you are. You must make peace with your brother. If you do not, you are not going anywhere in the rest of the areas of your life without great difficulty.

Evil Manifests

Evil spirits are alive. They are living beings. They just do not have a body. They are a spirit being just as real as God is. They are spiritual parasites. If you could look into the spirit world, you would see them just as surely as you are looking at me sitting in the physical world. They are alive spiritually. When they speak through you, it is the spirits using your vocal chords and your faculties to speak their intent. So when that old thing comes up and spouts out of your mouth, it was not you talking anyway. It was that evil spirit manifesting itself by its nature and using your faculties. your five physical senses, your vocal chords and your poor old brain. You went down, it came up. It spouts off and you get in trouble. Then it laughs at you.

I teach my kids spiritual things when they listen to that voice of rebellion and get into trouble. I look at them and I say, "You know what? That evil spirit is laughing at you because it got you in trouble. You are in trouble and it is having a heyday laughing at you, because that is its nature. It is going to try to get you in trouble all it can so it can manifest itself by its nature. Then when you are hurting, it is reminding you that it is having a heyday. Now, what do you want: do you want to have a good day or let it have a good day?" My kids say, "We would like to have a good day, Dad." I said, "Then you need to hold every thought in captivity."

That is how you teach young people spiritual things; they learn the thoughts of their own mind. **If the thoughts of your mind do not line up with the Scriptures, it is not of God.** There is no middle ground. The top of this fence is not 50 feet wide with you sitting on it. **You are either in the kingdom of God or you are in the kingdom of the devil,** *every minute of your day.* It is as simple as that. There is no neutral territory here.

The Word of God is coming to show you the very thoughts of your heart − to split you wide open, to x-ray you all the way to your toenails and to help you look inside and see what is not you. That which is not you has to go and you get to stay because this is your turf. God has created you to be on this planet, to rule it, subdue it and live in peace and rest.

If you have Rejection, you have an evil spirit. If you have Bitterness, you have an evil spirit. If you have Envy and Jealousy, you have the indwelling presence of an evil spirit.

When God created Adam and Eve, He said it was very good and there was no Bitterness, there was no Envy and Jealousy, and there was no Rejection. There was innocence. There was no evil.

Paul said in Romans, through one man sin entered into the world.

> **Wherefore, as by one man sin entered into the world, and death by sin; and so death passed upon all men, for that all have sinned:**   Romans 5:12

Sin came from somewhere else into the realm of man. It came from outside - from the spiritual dimension into the physical dimension in the realm of the spirit. The doors were opened, the floodgates were released and every being that fell with Lucifer poured into the second heavens surrounding this planet. That included fallen angels, devils, principalities and powers, spiritual wickedness in high places, and the rulers of the darkness of this world, all of them. They immediately had access to Adam and Eve, their children and their posterity, forever. They are still here today.

Legal Right

Do not be afraid of evil because the curse causeless does not come.

> As the bird by wandering, as the swallow by flying, so the
> curse causeless shall not come.   Proverbs 26:2

If you are serving God, there can be 14 million devils around you, yet they cannot touch you because there is no legal right. You give the devils a legal right yourself. Your ancestors did too. You gave permission. Somewhere in your life, your family or your ancestors cursed you, or someone opened the floodgates for these critters to come in and oppress you. Now the Lord has come that you might be free.

> ⁷For the earth which drinketh in the rain that cometh oft
> upon it, and bringeth forth herbs meet for them by whom it is
> dressed, receiveth blessing from God:
> ⁸But that which beareth thorns and briers is rejected, and is
> nigh unto cursing; whose end is to be burned.
> ⁹But, beloved, we are persuaded better things of you, and
> things that accompany salvation, though we thus speak.
>   Hebrews 6:7-9

This is an illustration of those that are following God and those that are not. Some people are like the fruit of the field of blessing of the grains, the crops, the plant and the corn, the wheat, the apples and all the stuff that we eat for our blessing, which we enjoy eating. Some people are another kind of fruit that bear thorns and briars and are rejected, nigh unto cursing. The only way to remove the bad fruit is to burn it. That is a type and a shadow of the Lake of Fire and the removal of evil from the earth that has been plaguing mankind.

Some people are so filled with Bitterness, Envy and Jealousy and Rejection that they are just like a briar bush and thorns. If you get around them they are going to bite you, kick at you, tell you to get lost, spit in your face, tell you to leave them alone. They are cursed and the only solution is for them to be burned. Now that does not happen quickly.

Eventually the fruits of Bitterness, Envy and Jealousy and Rejection can bring damnation to your soul by keeping you from the blessings of God and by keeping you from fellowship with God.

If you want to run on the wrong side of the road at 60 miles an hour, you are going to have a "malfunction in your junction" before the day is over with. If you continue to allow Satan to speak through you, act through you, use you, possess you and rule you in these areas, you are going to be like a car on the wrong side of the road. You are going to have a wreck. When you wreck you are going to blame everybody else but yourself because Rejection always blames someone else. Bitterness always blames someone else. Envy and jealousy always blames someone else. **Rejection always blames someone else – it never takes responsibility for its own actions.**

Cain and Abel

Let us take a look at what happens with rejection in the area of Cain and Abel.

> **¹And Adam knew Eve his wife; and she conceived, and bare Cain, and said, I have gotten a man from the LORD.**
> **²And she again bare his brother Abel. And Abel was a keeper of sheep, but Cain was a tiller of the ground.**
> **³And in process of time it came to pass, that Cain brought of the fruit of the ground an offering unto the LORD.**
> **⁴And Abel, he also brought of the firstlings of his flock and of the fat thereof. And the LORD had respect unto Abel and to his offering:**
> **⁵But unto Cain and to his offering he had not respect. And Cain was very wroth, and his countenance fell.**   Genesis 4:1-5

This is rejection by God.

There are many people who debate the situation with Cain and Abel. It seems to be, as we look at Cain, that he brought an offering from his crops, and it seems to be that Abel brought something very important – the firstling. A firstling would be the animal that would be without spot or blemish; it would be the best he had. He brought the fat, which meant that he had a sacrifice of burnt offering which would come up as a sweet smelling savor before God.

Anger is the first thing that happens in Rejection. If you have Rejection, the first thing that comes is Bitterness. Unforgiveness, Resentment, Retaliation, Anger and Wrath, Hatred, Violence and Murder come with Bitterness. Unless we have dealt with the elements of Bitterness, we cannot deal with Rejection.

Cain was rejected in his offering before God because he had offered just out of duty, not out of his heart. The difference between Cain and Abel is that Cain came out of duty and requirement, and Abel came out of his heart of worship - two men with two different natures. When Abel's offering was accepted of God over Cain's, Bitterness came to Cain.

If Cain had dealt with Bitterness already in his heart, when that spirit of Rejection came, he would not have regarded it. He would have said, "God, how come?" But he was wroth and the Lord said unto him, "Why are you angry, Cain? If you do well, shall not you be accepted?"

> **6And the Lord said unto Cain, Why art thou wroth? and why is thy countenance fallen?**
> **7If thou doest well, shalt thou not be accepted? and if thou doest not well, sin lieth at the door. And unto thee shall be his desire, and thou shalt rule over him.** Genesis 4:6-7

God had not rejected Cain because later on He goes down and says if you do not well, sin lies at the door and unto thee shall be his desire, and you shall rule over him. God is saying to Cain: "You just brought this sacrifice to Me because you felt you had to. It was not your first fruits that you brought. You came out of duty and religion.

I reject your offering, but I do not reject you. In fact, you still rule over Abel as the younger and you shall be his lord." God has not rejected Cain and his leadership nor had He rejected Cain as a person. He would only reject th e faulty offering of worship. But Cain took it personally and the first thing that came was Bitterness. Anger and Wrath came with Bitterness. Then he developed an attitude and his countenance fell.

Have you ever seen anyone in Rejection smile? Never. Have you ever seen anyone in Bitterness smile? Never. Have you ever seen anyone in Envy and Jealousy smile? Never. Discernment becomes very easy because we are seeing the external fruit of something internal. The ingredients of Rejection and Bitterness and Envy and Jealousy. What did Cain eventually do? Murder. The Scriptures are very clear in Genesis 4. God did not reject Cain as a man, and He did not reject him as a leader. He just rejected the faulty offering of worship.

Adam and Eve

The Word says that without the shedding of blood there was no remission of sins.

> **And almost all things are by the law purged with blood; and without shedding of blood is no remission.** Hebrews 9:22

When Adam and Eve sinned and ran off and hid in the woods and saw that they were naked, they covered themselves with fig leaves because they considered themselves unclean. The Lord came looking for them in the cool of the evening as was His custom, and He did not find them in the highways and the byways. He started calling for Adam, "Adam, where are you?" Adam said, "We are here." "Where?" "Out here in the woods."

And the Lord said, "**Who told you** that you were naked? **Who** gave you the knowledge that you were naked?"

> **And he said, Who told thee that thou *wast* naked? Hast thou eaten of the tree, whereof I commanded thee that thou shouldest not eat?** Genesis 3:11

The Bible says that the Lord killed an animal, took the skins and made clothing for Adam and Eve. He dressed them.

> **Unto Adam also and to his wife did the LORD God make coats of skins, and clothed them.** Genesis 3:21

That began the first instance of what would become the sacrifice of an animal with the shed blood under the Jewish law as a type and a shadow of the sacrificial Lamb that would eventually come. It represented God Himself coming to die for the sins of the beautiful people He created, who had become separated from Him because of Satan and sin.

Our Battle

> **Put on the whole armour of God, that ye may be able to stand against the wiles of the devil.** Ephesians 6:11

The word *wiles* is the Greed word **methodeia** (*Strong's #3180)*, which means methods, schemes, devices. This scripture is telling us to stand against the devices or the methods of the devil.

Jesus believes in the devil. He said, "I saw Satan fall like lightening from heaven." (Luke 10:18)

He took a stand against the devil. Paul said that many people are in opposition to themselves, because the devil has taken them captive at his (the devil's) will.

> **And that they may recover themselves out of the snare of the devil, who are taken captive by him at his will.**
> 2 Timothy 2:26

The devil is real; he is Lucifer.

> **For we wrestle not against flesh and blood, but against principalities, against powers, against the rulers of the darkness of this world, against spiritual wickedness in high places.** Ephesians 6:12

That word *wrestle* is the Greek word *palē* (*Strong's* #3823) and means warfare. Our warfare is not against flesh and blood.

When someone does evil to you, the thought comes very easily and very fast to make him or her evil in your mind. You retaliate against them with evil very quickly in return. Rejection always retaliates because it allows Bitterness to have an open door. Retaliation is the third underling of Bitterness. If Bitterness has not been dealt with, Retaliation is still able to manifest.

People can bump into your realities and your expectations and fail you. They may tell you something awful, they may reject you, they may defame you, or they may murder you with their tongue. They may do all manner of evil against you. You begin to think they are evil, and by labeling them evil, you let the devil off the hook. He is

16

laughing up a storm because now both of you are victims – you in your ignorance and the other person in their evil.

Your battle is not with what that person does to you. Your battle is with the principalities and powers in that person making them do what they are doing. God loves the person who does evil. God loves murderers. God loves homosexuals. God loves any person who is allowing evil spirits to operate through them. He hates the evil, but He loves the person. Evil separates that person from fellowship with Him and the relationship with Him because they make evil their god by choosing to allow the evil to rule them.

When you participate with evil, you make evil your god. Jesus said that to the Pharisees who said, "Our Father is Abraham and our Father is God." Jesus replied: "If your Father were God, you would do the works of your Father. Because you do not do the works of the Father, your father must be the devil." **Your battle is not with each other.**

> **[39]They answered and said unto him, Abraham is our father. Jesus saith unto them, If ye were Abraham's children, ye would do the works of Abraham.**
>
> **[44]Ye are of your father the devil, and the lusts of your father ye will do...**   John 8:39,44

The first requirement for you to be free, not just from Bitterness and Envy and Jealousy but also from Rejection, is that you are going to have to **separate the person from their evil**. You are going to have to exchange Rejection, Bitterness, Envy and Jealousy for compassion because that is the nature of your Father which is in heaven. He has compassion on them, not judgment. The days of judgment are not here. This is the age of grace and mercy.

Your battle is not with the people who have rejected you. Rejection is a sin. When you exchange the Bitterness, and the

Envy and Jealousy, and the Rejection for compassion, then you are like your Father, which is in heaven.

Rejection Defined

Rejection means to cast from one; to throw away; to refuse; to put aside. As a noun, the word rejection means a person or thing rejected as not up to some standard. The old English Latin derivative of rejection is *rejectare*. The *"re"* literally translated means back and the *"jectare"* means to throw. So rejection means to back-throw, to remove from your presence, to throw off.

Out of the Mouth...

Rejection always spouts off, Bitterness always spouts off, and Envy and Jealousy always has something to say. Give it time and it will say something.

Your Words

What comes out of your mouth establishes life and death to you. You can be thinking it in your heart, and it can be just temptation. When you speak it out of your mouth, you establish it in the heavenlies. The only one that can tear those words down is you. Your words are either life or death, blessings or cursings. You shall reap what you sow. If you sow unto death, you shall reap death. If you sow unto life, you shall reap life. Your reality is established by the words of your tongue.

The Bible says every word that has been spoken shall stand against you in the Day of Judgment.

> But I say unto you, That every idle word that men shall speak, they shall give account thereof in the day of judgment.
> **Matthew 12:36**

The Antidote

The only antidote to Rejection is repentance in your generation. You need to say,

> God, I repent. I pull those words down out of the heavenlies. I cast them down. I put them under the blood of Jesus for forgiveness of sins, and I ask to be delivered from the curse of my words.

That is the only way that you can be free of those words standing in condemnation and judgment against you in the judgment day.

What you speak must match your heart. What is in your heart should be the Word of God. What is in your heart should be what God has said about a matter. It is a conclusive statement about the final product of the thoughts of the inner man. The way you think on the inside should be what you speak out of your mouth.

The point I am trying to make is this: when you say to someone, "I hate you," you have established a spiritual dynamic that needs to be dealt with or else it stays there forever, waiting to be fulfilled. The object of Hatred is Murder. It is the final stage of the Bitterness.

The Lord Was Rejected

Isaiah 53 is a tremendous statement about our Lord and the prophecies concerning His coming. When the Lord came from heaven and became flesh, He was not surprised that He was rejected and murdered for your sins. The Lord knew it was going to happen to Him before it happened.

It is possible for you to know that you are going to be rejected in certain cases before it ever happens. If you are around certain people, that is your stressor in Rejection. If you are delivered from Rejection, you can face that person from then on and never be affected by it. If you have the spirit of Rejection and you face them, it will scare you. It will pierce you, and it will trouble you.

**You can stand
before any devil
and not be affected.**

The power of deliverance and the power of freedom is that you can stand before any devil and not be affected. You know the Bible says that the evil one came to Christ and found nothing within Him. He came to tempt Him; he came to find some way to get inside Jesus' spirit as a man. He did everything. He tempted Him and he caused persecution. Jesus was reviled even to death. The devil was waiting for Jesus to go into Bitterness, or Envy and Jealousy. The Bible says that the evil one came and found nothing within Jesus. He did not find any creature within His spiritual makeup, and that is why He is sinless.

> ... for the prince of this world cometh, and hath nothing in
> me. John 14:30

Isaiah prophesied by the Spirit of God that Jesus, when He came in the flesh as a man, would be rejected by men. Jesus did not take in an evil spirit of Rejection because of it. Neither do you have to take in that evil spirit. You do not have to be a pincushion for devils. You do not have to be a habitation of devils. You are supposed to be the temple of the Holy Ghost.

> ¹Who hath believed our report? and to whom is the arm of the LORD revealed?
> ²For he shall grow up before him as a tender plant, and as a root out of a dry ground: he hath no form nor comeliness; and when we shall see him, there is no beauty that we should desire him. Isaiah 53:1-2

This is a prophecy of Jesus coming in the flesh. He is despised and rejected of men.

> He is despised and rejected of men; a man of sorrows, and acquainted with grief: and we hid as it were our faces from him; he was despised, and we esteemed him not. Isaiah 53:3

There is your Lord: rejected of men. He went back to His church one Sabbath, stood up and read from the Scriptures as was His custom. He grew up in this church and stood up and read Isaiah 61, which was a prophecy of Himself.

> ¹⁶And he came to Nazareth, where he had been brought up: and, as his custom was, he went into the synagogue on the sabbath day, and stood up for to read.
> ¹⁷And there was delivered unto him the book of the prophet Esaias. And when he had opened the book, he found the place where it was written,
> ¹⁸The Spirit of the LORD is upon me, because he hath anointed me to preach the gospel to the poor; he hath sent me to heal the brokenhearted, to preach deliverance to the captives, and recovering of sight to the blind, to set at liberty them that are bruised,
> ¹⁹To preach the acceptable year of the LORD.
> ²¹And he began to say unto them, This day is this scripture fulfilled in your ears. Luke 4:16-19,21

He said, "This day are these words fulfilled in your ears." He was saying, "I am He." All His friends went and grabbed hold of Him and ran Him to the edge of the hill outside of

Nazareth to stone that poor Jesus to death in their rage and their anger. They were His peers in His home church. It says He passed through them and escaped from them (John 8:59). The Bible says a prophet is without honor in his own country (Matthew 13:57).

He was despised, rejected of men, a man of sorrows and acquainted with grief, and we hid as it were our faces from Him (Isaiah 53:3). His whole crew did that. Everyone abandoned Jesus at the cross. Peter denied Him openly and cursed and said he never knew Him. The rest of them peered around the telephone poles and the trees and said, "God, what is going on here." We hid our faces from Him.

He was despised and we esteemed Him not.

> **4Surely he hath borne our griefs, and carried our sorrows: yet we did esteem him stricken, smitten of God, and afflicted.**
> **5But he was wounded for our transgressions, he was bruised for our iniquities: the chastisement of our peace was upon him; and with his stripes we are healed.** Isaiah 53:4-5

The chastisement of our peace was upon Him. It means that we have been victimized by the devil, chastised of Satan, and that has been taken away from us and put on His back. Our peace was taken away because of sin. Now He has borne that sin. The chastisement that is coming upon us because of sin goes to Him, and we receive peace. We receive peace because He has taken the chastisement, and we receive the peace because He has made it possible.

> **6All we like sheep have gone astray; we have turned every one to his own way; and the LORD hath laid on him the iniquity of us all.**
> **7He was oppressed, and he was afflicted, yet he opened not his mouth: he is brought as a lamb to the slaughter, and as a sheep before her shearers is dumb, so he openeth not his mouth.** Isaiah 53:6-7

When He was being afflicted for you, He showed you the Spirit. He did not open His mouth. He was brought as a lamb to the slaughter. And as a sheep before her sheerer is dumb, so He opened not His mouth. He did not defend Himself in the rejection. He did not defend Himself in the bitterness and the murder. He did not defend Himself in the envy and the jealousy. He kept His mouth shut because He knew what was in their hearts.

We are not supposed to be victims. We are not to repay evil for evil. Under the law it was an eye for an eye, a tooth for a tooth (Leviticus 24:20). Jesus came not to defend Himself, but to defend us. It does not mean that we are to be a victim. It means that He took the penalty of this to show us that it was no longer an eye for an eye or a tooth for a tooth, but that we too should learn what was in the hearts of men. He did not defend Himself at all.

To say that we should be doormats is not scriptural either. There are many scriptures that say that a soft word or answer turneth away wrath (Proverbs 15:1). We are being shown the difference between God's heart and men's hearts. What He was doing was showing us the great infinite compassion even to death because of love. The Bible says,

> **Greater love hath no man than this, that a man lay down his life for his friends.**   John 15:13

Isaiah says,

> **⁸He was taken from prison and from judgment: and who shall declare his generation? for he was cut off out of the land of the living: for the transgression of my people was he stricken.**
> **⁹And he made his grave with the wicked, and with the rich in his death; because he had done no violence, neither was any deceit in his mouth.**

> ¹⁰Yet it pleased the LORD to bruise him; he hath put him to grief: when thou shalt make his soul an offering for sin, he shall see his seed, he shall prolong his days, and the pleasure of the LORD shall prosper in his hand.
>
> ¹¹He shall see of the travail of his soul, and shall be satisfied: by his knowledge shall my righteous servant justify many; for he shall bear their iniquities.
>
> ¹²Therefore will I divide him a portion with the great, and he shall divide the spoil with the strong; because he hath poured out his soul unto death: and he was numbered with the transgressors; and he bare the sin of many, and made intercession for the transgressors.   Isaiah 53:8-12

The Lord had to deal with Rejection. He had to deal with Bitterness. He had to deal with Envy and Jealousy. He showed it was possible to defeat it and not make it part of His life. In His strength as a work of the Holy Spirit, the Lord, the Father and the Holy Spirit will be there to meet you and remove that from your life so that you can be free from it and have your peace. Your peace can be complete because He understands what is happening on this planet.

You are going to have to have a perfect hatred for Rejection. You are going to have to make up your mind that you do not want it as part of your life anymore. If you do not, then when you are rejected, you will turn around and reject others. That will make you just as evil as the person who you do not like. It cannot be an eye for an eye and a tooth for a tooth.

If you do not deal with Rejection, it will go back into Bitterness, and it will go right back into the same dastardly deed that is being done to it. Now you have a vicious ping-pong, and the only person who loses is you. The devils do not lose; they are already judged. You lose and God does not want you to lose. He wants you to win.

Possible Open Doors for Rejection

Your Family Tree

You have the ability to remember when you were rejected. Many people do not remember anything of their childhood, but they are tormented by realities that are coming from their childhood. If you are tormented about something that you cannot remember, there would be evidence of a spiritual dynamic that would be suppressing you and then tormenting you beyond the realm of conscious thought. This would be something that we would pay attention to in our lives.

The source of your Rejection many times begins in your ancestry before you were ever conceived. The stage is set for a spirit of Rejection to come right into you because of the family history. There is much evidence of the rollover of spiritual problems in the Bible.

Abraham

One of the most famous examples of an inherited characteristic is in the case of Abraham, the father of our faith. When God called Abraham out of Ur of the Chaldees, Abraham had spiritual problems. This may shock you, but father Abraham was a liar. Father Abraham had Fear of man and he was a liar.

The Bible is very clear that he lied twice about Sarah being his wife. One time he lied to the Pharaoh about the identity of his wife. Then just after that, he lied to Abimelech, the king of the Philistines, about Sarah again. He did not learn the first time. He told the same lie again.

Because he feared, he said, "She is not my wife; she is my sister."

Therefore, Abraham had Fear of man. He had Fear of Rejection. He had Fear of failure. The root behind all people who lie is Fear of man, Fear of rejection, and Fear of failure.

Isaac

Interestingly enough, forty years later, Isaac, the son of Abraham, and his wife Rebekah went into the land of the Philistines. Abimelech was still king of the Philistines. The same king as when his father Abraham went there 40 years before. As Isaac and Rebekah came into the land of the Philistines where Abimelech was king, Isaac said the exact same words that his father did forty years before – word for word. He said, "She is not my wife; she is my sister" because he feared Abimelech would take his beautiful wife Rebekah. Who spoke out of Abraham? It was a spirit of Fear speaking through him. Who spoke through Isaac to Abimelech? It was a spirit of Fear speaking through him. Evil spirits are very boring, and they do not have much creativity when it comes to manifestation by their nature.

If you compare notes, you are all hearing the same voices saying the same things, from within yourself in various areas of your life – word for word.

**The root behind all people who lie is
Fear of man,
Fear of rejection and
Fear of failure.**

In the area of Rejection, voices that you might hear would be:

"You will never amount to anything."

"You are not important."

"You are a nobody."

"No one loves you."

Jacob

Isaac lied word for word just as his father Abraham did. We have two generations of liars, which are the fathers of your faith. Isaac had two sons, Jacob and Esau. Jacob and his mother Rebekah lied to Isaac about the matter of the birthright. Now we have a mother and her son in collusion lying to the father.

Now we have three generations of liars. We have Abraham, Isaac, and Jacob lying. Plus we have Sarah condoning it, we have Rebekah condoning it, and eventually participating with it.

Sons of Jacob

Jacob has twelve sons. Ten of these sons are liars too because they lied to their father about their Envy and Jealousy against Joseph in the case of the coat with many colors. They pretended he was eaten by a bear and showed their father the coat of many colors with blood all over it. Then they sold Joseph into slavery into Egypt.

Now we have ten more liars. We have four generations of liars. They are all the fathers of our faith. Full of fear and lying. That is just one example.

The point I am trying to make is this: a lying spirit or a spirit of Fear can be in your family tree before you are ever conceived. If a lying spirit was in the family tree of

Abraham, Isaac, and Jacob, then a lying spirit can be in your family tree. That also includes Rejection, and it is ready to come into you because Rejection is a sin. Rejection is a sin because it makes God a liar. It says you were an accident and you were a mistake.

However, Psalm 139 applies to every person on the face of this earth.

> **13For thou hast possessed my reins: thou hast covered me in my mother's womb.**
> **14I will praise thee; for I am fearfully and wonderfully made: marvellous are thy works; and that my soul knoweth right well.**   Psalm 139:13-14

This takes Rejection and trashes it because this indicates that God knew you before you were ever conceived. You are no mistake. You are no accident. It does not matter if you were conceived in sin. In your generation you belong here. You are here at the ordination of God from the foundation of the world and you belong here. He loves you with an everlasting love, and He is in joyful expectation of your future.

Rejection will steal that from you. Rejection will steal Psalm 139 from you. Rejection will steal Isaiah 45 from you. Rejection will steal your position with the Lord Jesus and with the Father. Rejection is a lie and Rejection makes God a liar.

Rejection is a liar and a thief.

If you follow Rejection in your personal life, it will make you a cohabiter with a liar, which is the devil. Your birthright and your inheritance are yours. You need to start accepting yourself as God has accepted you from the foundation of the world. Let God be true and every man a liar. When you listen to Rejection, you are making a lying man true and God a liar.

Your Family Tree

Rejection begins before you were ever born. Look at the spiritual dynamics of your life when you look back into your family tree. Start with yourself by drawing a box. Draw two lines from that box, one to represent your father and one to represent your mother. From each of their boxes draw two lines each to represent their father and their mother. Repeat this with every box until you have reached four levels deep. The third level represents your grandparents (4 boxes), and the fourth level your great-grandparents (8 boxes).

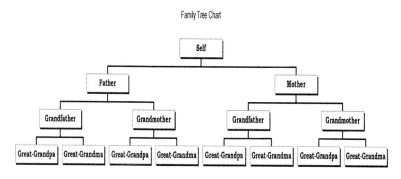

Family Tree Chart

When I am doing spiritual charts on inheritance, I go to the father first. When I go to the mother, I am looking back through her father. Every woman has a father too. I would trace it through the father every single time. If I were following this thing correctly, I would be following the curse down through the father of those females. I found it to be true most of the time.

Editor's Note: The Family Tree Chart tracking diseases is found in the *Study Guide* to accompany *A More Excellent Way*™.

Most people are in such denial and fabrication of personality, they do not even understand their own thoughts or their own fears. It is there in spite of them. This spirit of Fear goes into the fetus. It is not genetic. It is spiritual. It can come from a father or mother. When I look into inherited diseases, both spiritual and genetic, Exodus says the sins of the fathers shall be passed unto the third and fourth generations of them that hate me.

> Thou shalt not bow down thyself to them, nor serve them: for I the Lord thy God am a jealous God, visiting the iniquity of the fathers upon the children unto the third and fourth generation of them that hate me;   Exodus 20:5

It said, "the sins of the fathers." Now the women come along with their stuff too and they bring that into the family tree, but they bring it through their father. The children are the product of the spiritual dynamics, not only of their father, but their mother through her father, too.

We know certain things about our ancestry, and we know certain things that we have had to deal with in our life. We are privately breaking the ancestral curses that we are aware of off our children right up front, early. When we see them manifest, and we gather around the child and start dealing with them. If there is a spirit there, we cast it out. That is the kind of thing, when that child gets older, that child will not have to go through all this spiritual warfare that you and I are doing. If our parents did what we know now, they could have worked out the generational problems a lot sooner. We would have had a better life.

You can look back to your mothers and fathers and grandmothers and grandfathers and recognize Rejection in your family tree. You can see it today with brothers and sisters. You know what your families are dealing with. It helps you understand your family and possibly you can get the great exchange from bitterness to compassion done.

You know what your parents are struggling with. You know what your grandparents are struggling with. You know what killed them, if it was a disease. You know what is getting them today. You can read their mail. You can tell them the thoughts of their hearts because your eyes are opening to something called discernment.

So you have three problems.

1) You have the rollover from the genetics.

2) You have the rollover from the spiritual.

3) You have the rollover from the intellectual, which is the soul and the psyche of man.

Rejection in the Womb

Rejection can come in the womb. One way that an open door of Rejection can come is that mommy and daddy just find out that momma is pregnant. Several dynamics can happen: both parents are excited, both parents are not excited or one parent is excited and one parent is not excited.

When the parents know that the woman is pregnant, if there is no joy, and if that child is not recognized as belonging to God and given back to God immediately as a gift, Rejection will come in. The Bible says the children belong to God, not to the parents.

I talked to a lady the other day who way struggling with great Rejection. She said when her mother found that she was pregnant, she was not happy because the mother wanted to party for two or three years and have some fun; then maybe she would consider having a child. Within just a couple of months she was pregnant and she was not a happy camper. The moment that woman realized she was pregnant and had those feelings against that fetus that was just forming in the womb, there were spirits of Rejection, Abandonment, and Fear that immediately came in. Fear of Rejection, Fear of Abandonment, Unloving and unclean spirits were right there. Parents give the devil permission to come into mankind.

Inherited Realities

We know inherited genetic diseases are in the womb. Some babies are colicky and some are not. The babies that have colic have inherited Fear in the womb. I have ministered to babies that were colicky and cast the inherited spirit of Fear out of them. The colic went away and never came back.

Psychologists in the psychiatric industry today have also determined that facets of a person's personality can be inherited. They have observed that things like hatred, anxiety and so on can be inherited in family trees. Not just genetic defects can be inherited, but personality traits as well. Certain psychological diseases can be inherited without a genetic component being known whatsoever. Alcoholism can be inherited, but there is no genetic component they have been able to find yet. Molestation can be inherited, but there is no genetic component there either. Insanity can be inherited, and there can be an inherited genetic or spiritual component.

Manic depression is an inherited mental disease with a genetic component. It is a recessive gene through the mother in the 26th section of the X chromosome.

Paranoid schizophrenia can be inherited too, but there is no known genetic component. It is spiritual.

Adoption

I have not yet found an adopted child who did not have a spirit of Rejection. The child that is adopted will bring with him the spiritual curses of his natural biological family, regardless of the environment in the adopted family. They will bring the evil with them, spiritually and genetically, into that family. It is a shock. Psychologists like to tell us that environment shapes the child. Environment does not shape the child. It contributes to the welfare of the child. The child is shaped many times by the family history. That is the inherited component.

Adopted children are adopted for one or two reasons. The first reason is because of the death of a parent either from auto accident, or injury, or fire, or some calamity, or disease. They are orphaned.

The second reason is because a father abandons the family. The mother is not interested in raising the family and gives the child, or sometimes children, to a grandparent to raise. Thank God for the grandparents who raised orphans, but I have not found it to produce great spiritual strength. They are still adopted children even if it is the grandparents that raise them.

The child is sometimes given to a stranger. The history of foster homes is not very good in America for caring for orphans. You find most of your sexual abuse and your physical abuse being perpetuated on the children by the very people who were set in place to care for them.

Orphanages do not have a good reputation. I am sure there are good orphanages. I am sure there are good organizations that have fine programs for orphans. It is still a form of abandonment. I have found that all adopted children have Rejection.

The Second Child

I also have found that most second children in the family have Rejection. The second child can be the sandwich child. If a child is the second of three or more, the second child is the one that suffers most from Rejection. It could be the competition. It is a statistical reality. If you go into the psychiatric industry, they have observed it too. If you are a second child in the family, the chances of you having Rejection are very good.

However, if you are adopted, and you are adopted by God, then you are no longer rejected. The Holy Spirit is crying in your heart, "Abba Father." Jesus is crying "Abba Father" within you. The Spirit of the Father bears witness with your spirit that you are accepted of God, that you are sons and daughters. Rejection does not stand a chance.

When you allow Rejection to rule you, you are saying that your adoption by God was not true. You are casting away your heavenly Father, and you are going back under the bondage of the curses of your earthly father. In order to be free from your earthly father and his curses, you need to get under the provision of your Heavenly Father through Jesus Christ.

When you listen to Rejection, you are picking up the law. You are picking back up the beggarly elements of the world.

> But now, after that ye have known God, or rather are
> known of God, how turn ye again to the weak and beggarly
> elements, whereunto ye desire again to be in bondage?
>
> Galatians 4:9

You are picking back up the curse of abandonment. You are saying, "I am abandoned, I am rejected." God said, "No, you are not abandoned. I have accepted you. You are My son, you are My daughter." The Holy Spirit of God is crying out to you.

Because you are sons, God has sent forth the Spirit of His Son into your hearts crying, "Abba Father." Wherefore I am no more a servant, but a son or daughter, and if a son or a daughter, then an heir of God through Jesus Christ (Galatians 4:7). We have gone from an heir, child, servant, lord of all. We have cut right through it. If you are an heir and a joint heir with Christ through the Father, this entire planet and the entire universe is your turf. Wherever you put your foot is your turf because the Creator gave it to you. You lost it through Adam, and through Jesus you have taken it back. You are not a destroyer. You are a healer. You are a gift of God to mankind forever.

Conceived in Lust

Another open door for Rejection is being conceived in lust, not in love. David said,

> ...in sin my mother did conceive me.   Psalm 51:5

A few years ago I talked to a couple who were having terrible marriage problems. This guy went out and got drunk one night at the local bar. He woke up the next morning married to a woman he had met at the bar and got drunk with. Then they wondered why they were having marriage problems five years down the road! God did not put that marriage together. I have ministered to many people who were conceived in the atmosphere of a party spirit where parents ended up in a motel. There is a spirit of Rejection that comes in immediately because it is birthed in sin.

Many parents tell their children: "Did you know I had you by accident? I was out partying and got pregnant." A spirit of Rejection is right there looking for a way in. "What? You did not have me because of love?" "No, it just was an accident." That opens a door for a spirit of Rejection and lack of identity.

Bastard's Curse

Another open door to Rejection is the bastard's curse. That is not just Rejection. It is also a curse. The sins of the fathers in idolatry were to the third and fourth generation but to a child born out of wedlock, it is called the bastard's curse, and it goes to ten generations (Deuteronomy 23:2). To be considered a bastard, spiritually, means that a child was conceived out of wedlock.

Many people, whether they are married by the Justice of the Peace or married by a pastor, do not even like each other. The scripture says to obey the laws of the land. The laws of the land say that in order for you to be married and recognized, you have to go before a Justice of the Peace or a pastor, have a marriage certificate filed downtown in the courthouse and establish that on a particular date at a specific time you have married. If that is what constitutes a marriage in the United States of America, then we have to follow it for a marriage to be valid.

If a child was conceived before marriage, it would have been fornication and that would have been a sin. The child would have been born in sin because the Word, in the Old Testament and in the New Testament, forbids sexual relationships before marriage. If that is happening in your life, you are not going to be stoned at sundown. The Word says if you cannot behave yourself properly toward your virgin, you had better get married before you burn. That word *burn* does not mean hell. It means you continue to burn in your lust and your desire. It has to do with the burning of desire. It would be best for you to marry your virgin than to burn in lust towards her all the time. Get married. If you cannot behave yourself, get married. Basically you are sanctifying your lust. Now it is holy whereas before it was not, providing that lust was out of love, not out of lust.

The lineage of Jesus Christ includes a bastard. Perez was the son of Judah by his daughter-in-law Tamar. He was not married to her when he thought she was a prostitute on the side of the highway. She never did marry him. He said, "Your righteousness exceeds mine" because he violated the heart of God in posterity. It was important to God that Judah have a son by which the Messiah should come because the prophecy was this: that Shiloh would come out of the loins of Judah according to the flesh. The genealogy of Mary through her father Heli, back to Nathan, and back to Judah, and back to Adam tells that story in Luke 3.

The bastard's curse brings Rejection. Today the penalty for the curse has been paid and by appropriation a person can be free of the bastard's curse.

Gender

Rejection can come because a parent does not want the child because of gender – male or female.

Many parents, when they find out they are going to have a girl while they really want a boy, or the other way around, bring rejection upon that child. I have seen more families name their boys with female names, and their girls with male names just trying to bridge that. I have seen mothers dress their boys like little girls. It creates an identity crisis.

If we consider homosexuality, we might get into a whole range of Rejection from a mother or a father. It could go back to conception. It could go back to birth. It could go back to the very reality of instead of having a boy, they wanted a girl. Instead of having a girl, they wanted a boy. From my study of homosexuality and the identity crisis that comes with it and the need to be loved, it is rooted many times right in that area of Rejection by a parent in gender.

Many times a boy who goes into homosexuality needs a father. A girl who goes into homosexuality needs a father or a mother. They are seeking to satisfy the need for nurturing, the need for love. That unfulfilled need is not from God. It is an evil spirit that is capitalizing on the failure of someone to nurture that child. It can be a long time before the child even understands what is going on. It can be built into that child.

It is just like colic in children. A spirit of Fear is working right at conception. The baby does not have the process of thinking but within that child there is a spirit of Fear that is creating physiological problems, including dendrite manifestation which causes cramping. Many physiological problems are already beginning because of the indwelling presence of the inherited spiritual dynamic that is involved.

Rejecting Your Gender

Many men and women also do not want to be the male or female that they are. I have talked to many ladies who would prefer to be a man. Many men say, "I wish I were a female." Forget about the parents rejecting the child on that basis. There is a spirit that comes into certain people causing them to lose their identity, and they do not want to be what they are. That is Rejection, Self-Rejection.

Male and Female

The supposed supremacy of a male over a female is an issue we also need to deal with. That is a doctrine of devils coming out of hatred of a man. It has nothing to do with Rejection.

The conflict of a female wanting to be a man comes out of hatred for men. It would seem to be just the opposite, but it is not. The only way that you can defeat the hatred is to be what you hate because then you have dealt with it and conquered it. However, it does not work that way. In the Scriptures, through Christ in the New Covenant, there is neither bond nor free, Jew nor Greek, male nor female. In the New Testament time period, it levels it right out from a standpoint of gender. We are all the bride of Christ. Male and female, we are the bride of Christ. He is our spiritual husband forever.

Being a female is probably much easier in this generation because you do not have the judgment on your head that a man did in that day. He was given responsibility to care for creation and he did not. He is going to have to stand before the Lord and give an account as to why he did not take care of that female.

If you are female and do not want to be a female, you have an unclean spirit of Rejection and also a hatred of men. You need to repent to God. If you are a male and you really would prefer to be a female, you need to repent to God. If He wanted a female, He would have created a female. You are no accident. God did not make a mistake. No one is an accident. Even if you were conceived in sin, you were not an accident. God knew you would be conceived in sin because He knows your families. He knows what is coming down the family line. God is not surprised when a grandson is evil when He saw it coming down the fourth, fifth and tenth generation back. God knows that in a certain generation you might be born out of wedlock. It was no surprise to Him.

Competition

Rejection also can come because of competition. An insecure husband has a wife and he needs her. She is his source of identity. I have seen many men that cannot exist without their wives. The wives make all the decisions for them. They exist, but they cannot exist without their wife. In certain cases where a man is dependent upon his wife, he could resent the child that comes along.

When mommas have babies, they love on them. They spend time with them, they change their diapers, and they nurse them. They hold them, and they tell them how wonderful they are, how beautiful they are. They are supposed to do that. As the child is growing, the child requires a certain amount of attention. If the father feels rejected, he could resent that child. He could be subjected to Envy and Jealousy because of the attention that the child is getting that he wants. If so, there will be a spirit of Rejection transfer into the child from the father, even as a toddler.

Sometimes a mother will become jealous later on because of the daughter or the son's affection for the father. Parental rivalry is a form of Rejection. Sibling rivalry is also a form of Rejection. Rejection involves an identity crisis.

Sometimes the mother or father will go into child idolatry. Child idolatry is a very serious problem in America today. The child takes the place of the husband or the child takes the place of the wife. The child and the very reality of the child is the only thing that is important. That is ungodly government. It is the ungodly sequence of authority and government and positioning.

Some parents will give everything to a child, and they will spoil them. They will give everything because they say, "I want to make sure my child has all the things I did not have as a child." That is coming out of Fear. It is not good for your child to be spoiled.

There is nothing wrong with giving our children something. But there is a problem when we are into child idolatry, and we are controlled by the whims of it. A child wants everything. Or the child comes home and says little Johnny down the street has this from Wal-Mart, and he pitches a fit until you go buy it for him.

Being Parentless

Another open door for Rejection is growing up without a father or a mother. In blended families, sometimes the stepfather or the stepmother does not bring love into the home.

While the child is still very young another source of Rejection is a mother or a father dying. They grow up with knowing the father or mother was there but they died prematurely. So there is rejection from that parent. Many times in dealing with people, I find much hatred of God and the parent. I come across many adults and many children who hate their dead mother or dead father. Sometimes in ministry I have to get a person to forgive their dead mother or dead father.

The father is the most critical individual in Rejection. If you have ever struggled with God as Father, it is because a father has rejected you. If you couldn't trust your earthly father, how can you trust the Heavenly Father? So you have Fear of God, Fear of Rejection by God, Fear of failure concerning God. You do not trust God because you did not trust your earthly father.

The word *father* sometimes is not a good word. Sometimes the word *mother* is not a good word. Many diseases come out of Rejection by a mother. If your mother has rejected you, she was rejected herself. If your father has rejected you, he was rejected himself by parents. And if those parents rejected him, they were rejected also.

Defense Mechanisms

Rejection has defense mechanisms.

Withdrawal

What happens when you come up to a turtle while he is walking around? He withdraws into his shell.

The most important defense mechanism of Rejection is to withdraw like a turtle in the shell for protection.

One of the things that I hear in ministry trying to get people free is, "I am not going to allow myself to become vulnerable again. I am going to withdraw in a defense mechanism. I love the Lord, I love people, but they are not going to get close to me again. I am never going to allow myself to be put in a position where I can be hurt ever again." That is a common thought.

When Jesus came to the earth, the prophet Isaiah said in chapter 53 by the Spirit of God that Jesus was going to be murdered and He was going to be rejected and despised of men. He knew it before He came. He made Himself vulnerable and that is the standard.

Fear of Man

The reason for withdrawing like a turtle into its shell is Fear; Fear of man, Fear of woman, Fear of God. Fear of man will cause you to withdraw into your shell. You will run and hide. That is what Adam and Eve did when they sinned. They ran into their shell due to Fear of God. Some people are more afraid of man than they are of God. There are certain people not even afraid of God, but they are afraid of a man.

Fear of Failure

Another mechanism coming out of withdrawing like a turtle is Fear of failure. What did the Lord say about you? Though His bride fall, though she fall seven times, the Lord shall come along with His hand and lift them up and say, "Get up darling, let us go on now." He is saying to you by the Scriptures that you are going to blow it. You are going to fail Him, you are going to fail someone else, you may even fail yourself, but He is ready to go on. Fear of failure will not let you take any chances in relationship. Fear of failure will not allow you to take a risk.

Security is an illusion. There is nothing in life but opportunity. Security is fear. People are looking for security. They want security in their job; they want security in their health. That is Fear.

Fear of Rejection

In the area of Rejection, you lose the battle between your ears before you ever get to the war. You sit back and speculate about how many people are going to reject you today. When someone's face comes before your mind, you win and lose that battle right between your ears. That is Fear of Rejection. You might be surprised, but the person you are afraid of may be more afraid of you than you are of them.

Fear of Abandonment

Fear of abandonment is easily defeated when you read Isaiah 54. It says the Lord Himself has accepted you. No matter what your problem is. Isaiah 54 ought to be standard reading for you throughout all your Christian life. **Isaiah 53 and 54 are the foundation for freedom from Rejection**, because if God be for you, who can be against you?

You are betrothed; you are accepted. Your spiritual husband has accepted you even if you did not have it together, even if you were separated from Him, even if you had shame from your youth. He thinks you are pretty neat and He wants to be around you forever.

That is true. That is the bottom line. You say, "Yeah, but you do not know how many sins I am dealing with." He does and He still loves you. Who said sin had anything to do with love? All it says about sin is it will separate you from His love. He has not changed in His love; you have changed in yours. He is changeless. He says, "I change not." God does not change; He is consistently dedicated to the ideals that are best for you. He is consistently dedicated to you.

Adopted Children

There is always a spirit of Rejection that accompanies adopted children. It is there in spite of the surrogate parent. It is there in spite of the adopted child. There are forces and dynamics that are beyond the intellectual processes that interfere with the ability of the child to grow up with a safe feeling on the inside. That would give us much evidence of spirits at work. It also indicates the defense mechanisms Rejection establishes to protect its territory.

I remember the story of a world known minister and the son they adopted many years ago. They had a daughter and then they inherited a son and adopted him. They raised him in a very Christian atmosphere. He grew up at 17 to be a juvenile delinquent, a drug addict, much trouble; in and out of prison. They did not understand how that could happen. They raised the child in the nurture and admonition of the Lord.

But that child brought with him all the inherited spirits from his father and mother. The spirits were there at birth. They were there as a baby. As the child grew up, in spite of all the teaching and the environment that he was in, there were spiritual forces at work within him.

If you have forces within, they must manifest. A spirit will always manifest at some point, until it is dealt with. If a spirit has never been dealt with, then it still has a legal right. You need to go back and find out what the legal right is.

Heirs by Adoption

Rejection comes with adoption because the child has been abandoned or rejected by one or more parents. It is an open door. We are heirs by adoption.

Rejection can came because of abandonment. You are separated from your natural parents, either by death or by spirit. You are separated from your natural parents because spiritually they are opposed to you. If you are separated from your natural parents because they are not in fellowship with you, then you have abandonment, you have fear, and you have Rejection.

Galatians 4 reminds us:

> **4But when the fullness of the time was come, God sent forth his Son, made of a woman, made under the law,**
> **5To redeem them that were under the law, that we might receive the adoption of sons.**
> **6And because ye are sons, God hath sent forth the Spirit of his Son into your hearts, crying, Abba, Father.**
> **7Wherefore thou art no more a servant, but a son; and if a son, then an heir of God through Christ.**   Galatians 4:4-7

Adoption by God has freed you from the Rejection of man. If a parent abandoned you and you were an adopted child, it did not break the Rejection. But when God has adopts you, it breaks the Rejection because He is the One who created you. He has redeemed you back to Himself in spite of the failure of any other person created, including your biological parents.

God was no longer our Father when we sold our soul to the devil under the curse of Adam and Eve. All of mankind has been separated from God from that point and needs to be restored to God spiritually as a spiritual Father.

Being Born Again

When we died spiritually and sin became part of our nature, God no longer was our Father. That is why we must be born again. Jesus said you must be born again.

It means that we accept God's forgiveness because of our separation from sin historically and personally. As a work of the Holy Spirit, our spirit comes alive to God whereas it was dead to God. We are redeemed. We are restored to Him because He is our real Father, but He lost us to death.

The wages of sin is death. God adopts us while we are sons of the devil. We are sons of the devil spiritually, not genetically; that is a human characteristic. We are separated from God, and the devil has been our father spiritually. Through water baptism we fall out of agreement with that lie. Water baptism is acknowledging that you are dead to that old man, Satan, your father. You are dead to what he stands for and you have been raised in newness of life. You are a new creature, a new creation. We are now adopted by the Father, restored back to Him.

We blew our inheritance. We turned away from God in our generations. We made the devil our spiritual father and served him, and we told God to get lost. In that day we died spiritually and needed a Savior. That is the whole purpose of Christ's coming. He said, "I came to show you the Father." Why? We had become separated from the Father because of sin. When we talk about adoption, we are now a new creature. Father God has adopted us out of the world of Satan. Thereby we can cry out - Abba Father. Galatians 4 says God has sent forth the Spirit of His Son into your heart crying Abba Father. You are no more a servant, but a son, if a son then an heir of God through Christ Jesus.

Romans reiterates this.

> For ye have not received the spirit of bondage again to fear; but ye have received the Spirit of adoption, whereby we cry, Abba, Father.   Romans 8:15

If Rejection came into us by abandonment by a parent, how do we get rid of the Rejection coming from adoption? We get rid of it by the Father. He takes the Rejection from us. He does it because of what Jesus did to make it possible to be free of these principalities and powers that are binding us in separation from God and from man and from each other and from ourselves.

Exploding with Anger and Hatred

The second defense mechanism of Rejection is exploding with anger and hatred.

When a person has a spirit of Rejection they are capable of being a bull in a china closet. Sometimes they do not withdraw like a turtle. Sometimes they become very aggressive with exploding anger, spouting off, chewing you up one side and down the other. They are exploding with anger and hatred, and they are fighting bitterly against real or supposed injustice or pain.

There are two ingredients of Rejection: it really did happen to them or they imagined it. Many people deal with Rejection, which they just made up in their heads. The person really did not reject them at all, did not really have anything against them, but because they have a spirit of Rejection, they take every little word, every little look, every little sight, sound, smell, word, whatever and twist it and turn it to make them rejected. Then they explode with anger and bitterness.

We have Rejection coupled with a root of Bitterness when you see someone exploding in anger and rage. Whenever you find any of these spirits that make up the armor of Bitterness from the lesser to the greater, you will find everything behind it there. When you find Anger and Wrath, you have Retaliation. You have Resentment. You have Unforgiveness. You have Bitterness. If Anger and Wrath are left unchecked, it will go to Hatred. If Hatred is left unchecked, it will go to Violence. If Violence is left unchecked, it will go to Murder. Now we have Rejection being reinforced and fueled by Bitterness. A defense mechanism for Rejection is Bitterness. **Rejection is now hiding behind Bitterness.**

A bully has a spirit of Rejection and he covers it up with bravado. He covers up with the defense mechanism called bravado so you will not see that he is full of Fear. A bully is a very insecure person and has the need for an identity.

Looking for Identity

A third defense mechanism of Rejection is looking for a meaningful identity outside of a true and complete relationship with the Godhead: the Father, the Word who is Jesus, and the Holy Spirit. When you read Isaiah 54, if you are complete in the love of God the Father, if you are complete in the love of the Lord Jesus, if you are in fellowship with the Holy Ghost, you have your identity because Isaiah 54 says you are the bride of Christ.

Rejection will not allow you to have an identity. If you come along and try to force the issue, what is behind Rejection is that there is no identity. Rejection does not want you to find yourself because if you ever find yourself and you ever know who you are, Rejection does not stand a chance. Rejection cannot stand before a true identity that comes from God because God, the Holy Spirit, is there to confirm that identity. When you line up with God's identity in your life, you have the Godhead with you. God has not given you the spirit of Fear. Fear is rooted in Rejection.

Identity crisis is a big deal. If people did not have an identity crisis, we would not sell so many self-help books to build you up in who you are. Why do you need to build yourself up in who you are? You already, by faith, are the best thing that ever happened in creation. You have arrived, by faith. You know who you are.

You are being prepared by the Father as a work of the Holy Spirit to be presented to the Lord Jesus as a bride without spot or blemish. You are just like Queen Esther. You are being prepared for that day to be presented to the King of Glory as a bride without spot or blemish. You are betrothed to the Lord!

Using Others as Your Source

Sometimes the identity crisis or establishing a meaningful identity is that you want to pattern yourself after some other human being as a role model. There is nothing wrong with role models, but there is something wrong with idolatry. Paul said, "Emulate me as I emulate Christ within me." Paul said, "The things that I do, I do because I follow Christ. Follow Christ as I follow Christ. Emulate the Christ that you see in me."

I have seen people who could not exist unless they had someone else beside them at all times to support them in their life. A beautiful girl who has Self-Rejection finds another friend who way uglier than she is to be her friend.

Why doesn't the beautiful girl find someone more beautiful than she is? Because she is intimidated – she already has Self-Rejection and Self-Hatred.

You stand alone before God and your identity needs to be complete in Him. You do not need anyone else to have an identity. He is your identity.

You know the old saying "Birds of a feather flock together" is very true. I have found that people who only want to talk about themselves will hang out with other people who just want to talk about themselves. That is the basis of all support groups.

Fabricated Personalities

A few years ago I ministered to a man who grew up in an atmosphere where his father would take him to porno studios when he was seven and eight years old. His father would follow the carnivals. His father was a loser who never made much money and bounced from town to town. This young boy had such contempt for his father that he purposed in his heart that when he grew up, he would be just the opposite of his father.

He came to me at age 34 as a successful businessman. He was tormented day and night. He was a believer, married with children, loved God, loved Jesus, a saint all the way. In a ministry session we found out he did not exist. The real man did not exist and what we had was a fabricated personality. He had made a mental list of the 37 attributes of his father that he hated. He went ahead and did just the opposite of the 37 things he hated in his father. So he was in 37 points just the opposite of his father and that is who he was. But is that really who he was? No wonder he was tormented. He did not exist.

Multiple personalities come to mask and to hide the hurt. A person can have as many multiples as it requires to cope with the pain. There could be five, ten, fifteen, or many more personalities. Some of them come with names that come up to help that person live their life.

Fabricated personalities can be called manic depression, they can be called paranoid schizophrenia, they can be called multiple personality (MPD), they can be called schizoid, or they can be called psychotic.

Editor's Note: MPD is now called dissociative identity disorder (DID).

Spirits Intertwined with Rejection

Our enemy comes and entwines himself in our lives.

If it was just a simple dealing with Rejection, we could deal with him by himself. But he is interlocked with a braiding, an interlocking and an interweaving, a mixing together of entwining of other realities. Fear intertwines itself to Rejection.

Rebellion intertwines itself to Rejection.

Fear of Rejection intertwines itself with Fear and Rejection.

Fear of Man intertwines itself with Fear and someone else.

Fear of Failure intertwines itself with Rejection, Fear and taking thought for tomorrow.

Fear of Abandonment intertwines itself with Fear, Rejection and distrust. When you get into distrust, you get into a lack of faith, you get into unbelief and you get into doubt. It is not possible to believe if you have doubt and unbelief.

Rejection could be held in place by other realities that need to be dealt with also. Sometimes Rejection will not be that easy to pry loose if we do not identify some of the other bondages and entwining that need to be recognized.

Fruits of Rejection

Barrenness

Isaiah says,

> Sing, O barren, thou that didst not bear; break forth into singing, and cry aloud, thou that didst not travail with child: for more are the children of the desolate than the children of the married wife, saith the LORD. Isaiah 54:1

This deals with barrenness. Many ladies are barren and are full of Rejection. They feel rejected by God. They feel rejected by their husbands. They have Self-Rejection. They have Self-Hatred. They have Guilt because they have never been able to bear children. Rejection and Fear of Rejection, Self-Hatred and an Unloving spirit will produce barrenness.

Miscarriages

Understand that many miscarriages are the result of an autoimmune problem in which the white blood cells are attacking the umbilical cord, causing a proliferation of white blood cells producing swelling and edema and a closure. They keep the blood, the oxygen and the nutrients from getting into the placenta and into the fetus. The child is actually asphyxiating itself in the womb and dies, and that produces the miscarriage. That is coming out of Self-Hatred and Self-Rejection.

We know anxiety and fear can produce frigidity and impotence. Fear can produce barrenness. Your endocrine system is a responder to your spiritual realities. Your ovaries are part of your endocrine system if you are a female. The sexual glands of male and female are part of the endocrine system. In the same way your thyroid can malfunction because of anxiety and fear, or your pineal gland can malfunction and under-secrete serotonin because of Self-Rejection, so can sexual glands over- or under-secrete. The whole biological processes of procreation can be affected.

Shame

Shame, the unloving, unclean spirit comes with Rejection. The following feelings also come with Rejection: "I do not feel like I belong. No one loves me. They are just lying to me. I know I am no good. I know I do not belong here. Oh, do not look me in the eye. I cannot stand it when you do that. Do not tell me I am loved. I am not worthy. I am guilty. I am no good. I am so full of shame."

In some cases, Rejection and Shame will take you to addictive drugs just to kill the pain of it. That is the root behind all addictions. You just cannot stand the feelings of Rejection and Guilt and Shame so you need a chemical fix. The root for all addictions is Fear, Shame, Guilt and Rejection. There is the need for an identity.

Editor's Note: The root of all addictions is also the need to be loved. *Addictions* is recommended and can be purchased from the Be in Health™ bookstore.

"For you shall forget the shame of your youth" (Isaiah 54:4). You do not have to live with that inherited stuff from your mother's womb. You do not have to live with that rejection from childhood. You can forget the shame and the rejection and the guilt from your past. The devil says, "I know what you did when you were 17. Do you want to talk about that abortion? Do you want to talk about that little relationship you had? Do you want to talk about this and that?" When you hear those voices coming, why don't you say, "Excuse me! Would you just mind going up to the throne and telling Father what you are telling me in my head right now and see what He has to say about it?" I have not found a devil yet that will go up to the Father and confront Him. I have asked them to.

You have to know who you are.

> **Wherefore thou art no more a servant, but a son; and if a son, then an heir of God through Christ.** Galatians 4:7

You are accepted of God. You may be despised and rejected of men, but you are accepted of God in heaven.

> I am an heir. Oh, bless God. I am a daughter of
> God. I am a son of God. God has accepted me.

Shame is saying, "Shut up." Rejection said, "No you are not," and everything is raging on the inside of you. The Word says, "I am the righteousness of God in Christ Jesus."

One of the greatest things
that helps
get rid of Rejection
is confession.

The Bible says,

> **Confess your faults one to another, and pray one for another, that ye may be healed. The effectual fervent prayer of a righteous man availeth much.** James 5:16

55

Confess your rejections, confess your bitterness, and confess your stuff. Bring it into light that you may be healed. Rejection will not allow you to deal with your stuff.

Run and Hide

Rejection, Shame, Fear of God, and Fear of Rejection caused Adam and Eve to run into the bushes and hide. It will cause you to run somewhere and hide also. When you are hiding, you are not in faith or in peace. You are in fear.

I will never forget one time when I was a kid. It was a big thing to drive the tractor. We used to harvest potatoes in the fall, and we would make all of our money for clothes and other items at that time of the year. I was probably 15 years old. We would go between fields, and they would have the tractor with a big cart behind it. They would pick potatoes, put them in barrels and take them to the potato house.

I kept thinking, "If the farmer would just let me drive the tractor..."

We had this big Farmall tractor with big double wheels, not the little narrow ones like a John Deere, but the wide ones. One day I had a chance to drive the tractor between fields. I was driving the tractor between fields a little slow and doing a nice job. Back in those days with those old tractors there was something they never told you. If you did not turn those old tractors off in a certain way after you turned the key off and you stopped, if you did not set the clutch and the ignition just right, they would burp on you and lurch. That kind of tractor had an after burp.

I pulled up in this field next to a beautiful 1955 Chevrolet Belaire that was gray and pink that belonged to an older couple. That car was like brand new. It was a sharp '55, gray and pink. I pulled up next to it carefully, took my foot off the clutch, turned the key off, sat back relaxed. I did it! I drove from field to field. All of a sudden it did its famous lurch burp; right into the side door of the '55 Chevrolet! I looked up and the door was caved in. I was like Adam and Eve; I headed for the woods and I did not come out. My father finally found me in there somewhere, and I wished I could have stayed in the woods.

Rejection will not let you deal with the problem. It will not let you face the problem. It will cause you to run and hide.

Spiritually Widowed and Spiritually Fatherless

Isaiah says,

> ...and thou shalt not remember the reproach of thy widowhood any more.   Isaiah 54:4

This is in the context of our relationship with God. There is a three-dimensional approach to this scripture. There is the statement between God and His people back then. There is a statement between God and His people in the future. There is a literal spiritual approach to you and your relationship to God personally right now, today.

One of the things I deal with in ministry is Rejection of the woman by her father and by her husband. Both the man as father and the man as husband represent God the Father and God the Word, who is Jesus.

When we have a violation of a woman's relationship with her father, it separates her not just from her earthly father, but also from her Father God. There are spirits that come to make sure this happens. The Fear of her father is transferred to Fear of God.

If a husband violates his relationship with his wife and is not to the woman as Christ is to the church, then the woman has a fear of Jesus. She has a fear of the husband, she has a fear of Jesus, she has a fear of God, she does not feel loved and there is Rejection.

This ministry deals with many females whose fathers are still alive and whose husbands are still alive, but the father and the husband might as well be dead because they leave them spiritually fatherless and a widow spiritually. I work with females who are married but there is no connection between them and their husband. She is a spiritual widow. I work with females whose fathers are alive, but there is no connection between them and their father whatsoever. He is spiritually dead. Spiritually, she is fatherless. Whether the father is alive or dead, whether the husband is alive or dead, does not make any difference. The spiritual dynamics are still the same. We have someone dead in the relationship.

For thy Maker is thine husband... Isaiah 54:5

The Creator is God the Word. John says God the Father created all things through Jesus Christ the Word. Paul says God the Father created all things visible and invisible through Jesus Christ the Word. Paul said that God the Father created all things visible and invisible, whether it be heaven or in earth, principalities and powers visible and invisible, through Jesus Christ when He was in heaven as the Word.

[1]In the beginning was the Word, and the Word was with God, and the Word was God.
[2]The same was in the beginning with God.
[3]All things were made by him; and without him was not any thing made that was made. John 1:1-3

Hath in these last days spoken unto us by his Son, whom he hath appointed heir of all things, by whom also he made the worlds; Hebrews 1:2

> For by him were all things created, that are in heaven, and that are in earth, visible and invisible, whether they be thrones, or dominions, or principalities, or powers: all things were created by him, and for him: Colossians 1:16

God the Father *willed* it, but it was God the Word that *spoke* it into being, and it was God the Holy Spirit that *did* it.

Scripture says it in Genesis 1, Isaiah 42, Isaiah 45, Isaiah 48, John 1, Colossians 1 and in Hebrews 1. The Creator who spoke everything into existence out of nothing was God the Word; we know Him as Jesus Christ.

> Thus saith God the LORD, he that created the heavens, and stretched them out; he that spread forth the earth, and that which cometh out of it; he that giveth breath unto the people upon it, and spirit to them that walk therein: Isaiah 42:5

> [1]In the beginning God created the heaven and the earth.
> [2]And the earth was without form, and void; and darkness was upon the face of the deep.
> [3]And the Spirit of God moved upon the face of the waters. And God said, Let there be light: and there was light.
> Genesis 1:1-3

> I form the light, and create darkness: I make peace, and create evil: I the LORD do all these things.   Isaiah 45:7

> I have declared the former things from the beginning; and they went forth out of my mouth, and I shewed them; I did them suddenly, and they came to pass.   Isaiah 48:3

That is why it is so important for you to be restored to Him and why it is so important for you to be restored to the Father through Him so that the fullness of the Godhead can be part of your relationship again.

Your Spiritual Husband

Spiritually and mystically, not in the carnal sexual sense, but in the correct spiritual sense Jesus Christ is your husband. That is why you are called the bride of Christ. You are the helpmeet - male and female - all of us, eternally. You will follow the Lamb, follow your spiritual Husband into eternity and forever rule the nations. Jesus is your husband.

Your Husband created you, and He stepped off His throne in heaven and came down to this planet that has been damned because He loved His wife who was dying. How in the world can Rejection stand a chance? How can Rejection stand a chance if you allow God the Holy Spirit to give you the revelation of this kind of acceptance and love? Jesus died for your sins and He came to get His beautiful wife who was dying in the pits of Satan's jaws because He loves you. And it was not just Him loving you. John 3:16 says it was the Father who sent Him.

> For God so loved the world, that he gave his only begotten Son, that whosoever believeth in him should not perish, but have everlasting life. John 3:16

The Father loves you. Jesus loves you.

The spiritual breach of your widowhood is healed forever. The spiritual breach of your fatherhood (no father present) is healed forever. That is why a father can heal you of Rejection. That is why a husband can heal you of the Rejection, because in literal reality your real father is God and your real husband is Jesus. No one else counts. In eternity it will not be your literal genetic father, or your literal husband that is important anyway. It is the Father and it is Jesus, and if you make your peace at that level now by faith for the future, it shall be executed now.

You say to Rejection:

> Stop interfering with my relationship with my Father. Stop interfering with my relationship with my husband Jesus. Stop interfering with

my fellowship with the Holy Ghost. Stop interfering with my fellowship with myself. Stop interfering with my fellowship with others. Rejection, you have to go in the name of Jesus.

For the LORD hath called thee as a woman forsaken and grieved in spirit, and a wife of youth, when thou wast refused, saith thy God.   Isaiah 54:6

For the LORD, that is Jehovah who is Jesus, has called thee as a woman forsaken and grieved in spirit.

Grieved in spirit is Rejection. Being forsaken is Rejection. Who is calling to you in your Rejection from your youth? The Lord is calling for you. He loves you. You are not rejected.

Many females feel forsaken and are grieved in spirit. **That is the root of many of your diseases.**

I do not know if you are fighting Rejection from time to time, but Isaiah 53 will give you someone who faced it. Isaiah 54 will show that you are right behind Him. Isaiah 53 shows the Lord in rejection, but He has defeated the spirit of Rejection. He is talking about redeeming the rest of us who have been desolated by Accusing spirits, Rejection, and Unloving spirits. He is telling you if you have ears, "Rejection, you do not stand a chance because if God be for me, who can be against me?" Why should you live in Rejection? You ought to hold your head high.

Are you going to finally accept yourself once and for all?

Father, I repent for listening to a lying spirit in my life. God I want to be delivered. I do not want to wait. Today is the day of salvation. I was given the Word that gives me the insight into my acceptance by You, God. I am not rejected.

The Word says, "But the shame of my past shall be taken away." Say to yourself:

I am clean by the blood of Jesus. I have been freed by my Husband, by faith. He loves me. He came to get me. I am in my birthright. I am out of my shame. I am in my element as a son or daughter of God.

Rebellion

Rebellion is a fruit of Rejection. You would never have rebellion if you were accepted. If you want to stop rebellion in children, it has to begin with acceptance, but it has to begin early on. It has to begin with parents who have spiritual understanding and can break the curses of inheritance and get involved with that child.

If the mother is pregnant with a child, the parent should begin breaking the curses immediately upon knowledge of conception. Come before the Lord, acknowledge what is in the family tree and get involved. You would be surprised how productive that will be when that child is born. Most of us were never taught spiritual things.

If a parent says, "Do not do as I do, but do as I say," you have had it. That is an open doorway for rebellion because it is a double standard. It is double minded, and the child will lose all respect. Obedience comes out of respect. Rebellion comes out of no respect.

> My son, hear the instruction of thy father, and forsake not the law of thy mother:
>
> Proverbs 1:8

When the children do not obey the law of the mother, the mother in my family says, "If you do not start to do this, then I will have to go to your father." They do not want that to happen because they know that I will act and I will get involved and they will have to conform to whatever that image is for our family unit or school unit. They know I will do exactly what I say I am going to do. That is now a pattern, and they have respect.

Following False Religions

The fruit of Rejection is pretty interesting. People follow false religions, false prophets, false teachers and churches that lead people astray because they have no identity. False prophets are established because they have no identity. Divination comes up in people who have no identity. The devil wants to give you a counterfeit for God's identity. The devil wants to give you an identity because he is the one that stripped you from your identity. Then he comes along and gives you another one that is of his liking, but it includes a perversion.

Individuals who have no identity develop false religions and cults. People who follow them are people who have no identity and are looking for an identity because of Rejection. They are looking for a state of being.

What God is doing with you and the reconstruction of you should happen to the degree that you will develop without any concern about it. If you are concerned about who you are in the church, you have an identity crisis. If you are concerned about your position in the church, you have an identity crisis. You have Rejection.

Wrong Desire for Spiritual Gifts

Another fruit of Rejection in the church is a wrong desire for spiritual gifts as a means of securing status and recognition. These desires are motivated because there is Rejection and lack of identity. There is something within them, which is Rejection, saying: "I want to be known." They want to be known as "the known ones" in the midst of the lesser ones.

I know who I am. I am just the first amongst equals. It gives me no preeminence at all. That is what the Word says I am, as a leader. You are sheep, but I am a sheep too. I am a sheep of God's pasture. In the midst of you, God has raised me up to be a slave to you. If you want to know my identity: I am a slave of Jesus Christ and I am your slave. I am your servant. That is my identity. I am the bridge that you run on. I am the highway that you trample. That is how important I am.

People who have Rejection do not want to serve. They want to be recognized. They want to sit in the seats of preeminence. They want to be called sir and ma'am.

It is amazing today that we have so many DDs, ThDs, DDTs, ABCs, XYZs after the names of leaders of God's people. Now it is Doctor so-and-so. When I read Matthew, Mark, Luke, John and the book of Acts, they just called Jesus, "Jesus." They just called Paul, "Paul,'" and they just called Peter, "Peter." Where did this reverend business come from? Where did this doctor so-and-so come from? That is coming out of need for recognition.

The need for recognition
reflects Rejection and lack of identity.

What did they call Jesus for a title? Teacher and Rabboni, which means teacher. They did not call Him "Right Reverend." They did not call Him "Doctor." They did not call Him "Father." In fact the Bible says to call no man "father." Call Him "Father God."

False Prophecy and Divination

There is something else in the church coming out of Rejection, and that is false prophecy and divination, which is words of knowledge that are soulish.

God said in the book of Jeremiah that the prophets prophesied out of their own spirits. There is a difference in prophesying out of your spirit versus prophesying by the Spirit of God. If you prophesy out of your own spirit, it is just you talking. When you prophesy by the Spirit of God, it is the Holy Spirit speaking through you. There is a big difference between the Holy Spirit speaking through you, and you speaking out of your own spirit.

Rejection produces matriarchal control. It produces legalism. It produces Pharisaism. Any need for identity and the need to be accepted by man are rooted in Rejection. If you need someone else's approval, then you have a spirit of Rejection. If you are watching someone's facial features, as to whether they are smiling at you or they are not smiling at you, then you have Rejection. If you are following someone around with your eyes to see if they notice you or they do not notice you, then you have Rejection. If you care about what other people think about you and meditate on it, then you have Rejection.

Insight into Insanity

In the area of Rejection we have an insight into insanity. Modern day psychologists say that sanity is relative and there are no longer any sane people in the world. That is good news because now we can fellowship together in our insanity and that is a degree of normalcy.

Insanity includes the three areas of Fear, Rejection and Rebellion. Remember that Rejection includes Fear of man, Fear of rejection, Fear of failure and Fear of abandonment.

We use 1 John in the healing of many fear-related diseases. There are four parts to this scripture.

> **There is no fear in love; but perfect love casteth out fear: because fear hath torment. He that feareth is not made perfect in love.** 1 John 4:18

1) There is no fear in love. If you are being loved, there is no fear. If you are not being loved, fear comes. 2) Perfect love casts our fear. You have fear that is producing Rejection and this scripture says perfect love casts out fear. Love is perfected when you love God, love yourself and love your neighbor as yourself. Perfect love casts out fear.

The beginning of the healing of all insanity is receiving the love of God. Paul says,

> **For God hath not given us the spirit of fear; but of power, and of love, and of a sound mind.** 2 Timothy 1:7

If you do not have fear, you have a sound mind. If you have fear, you do not have a sound mind. 3) Fear hast torment. Without a sound mind, you have insanity (mental problems) and torment in the mind. Insanity is a result of a breakdown in human relationship, both inherited and personal. Insanity is a result of fear.

Insanity
is a direct result
of involvement with the occult.

A person will run to the occult because they do not believe in God. They want a different god. They want to create their own love. They may say, "Let us make love, not war." When we look at recent history, that approach did not work very well. The Bible says when they say peace, peace, then comes sudden destruction. Man - made peace and man - made love does not work. Peace with God is where it begins because He is our source. You have to have your peace with God in the area of love before you can ever love yourself or you can ever love others. It is not possible without that.

We are saying, "If other people would love me, then I could love myself. If I could love myself, then I could love and receive the love of God." Mankind trying to heal himself is the opposite of the truth. He is thinking that, "If I could make peace with my brother, then I will have a better day. If I have a better day because I have peace with my brother, then I feel accepted of God." That is exactly the mentality, but that is not correct. You go to God first. Even when you are still unhappy with yourself or at odds with your brother, you go to the Father first and take care of it. Then His love flowing through you will work out the rest. It has to go there first.

Because you feel unclean, because you feel unworthy, because you feel rejected, because you feel guilty, because you have Self-Rejection and Self-Hatred, you *feel* the Father is mad at you. You *feel* that He does not love you and He does not like you if you go to Him in your present state of feelings. You know the feelings your brother has for you and you have for him and you know how you feel about yourself. You do not go to the Father because you are afraid of Rejection from the Father because you are exposed to your unloveliness and because you *feel* He is going to reject you. That is expectation of rejection by a father, this time, by God the Father.

That is Rejection. The antidote is to come boldly before the throne of grace in time of need.

4) He that feareth is not make perfect in love himself. This would be because of Rejection, Fear, and Fear of Rejection. If you have Fear, if you have Rejection, if you have torment, you are unable to give and receive love yourself. If you are unable to give and receive love, then you are unable to love yourself and you are unable to love others and receive their love.

An insight into insanity is that it includes the need for men's approval and dependency on others. Rejection by others is a wound to the spirit because Rejection is a spirit. It is not a wound to the intellect although the intellect will remember the wound. Intellectually through your memes and memory, you remember the wound. However, it is not the memory that is causing the problem. It is the evil spirit within your spirit that is causing the problem.

It is amazing that when people are delivered from Rejection, they remember when they were rejected but they no longer have the feeling or the pain. When you have not been delivered from Rejection, you have the memory and you have the pain. You think it in your head, and you feel it in your spirit.

The wounding of the spirit is the entrance into the human spirit by an evil spirit representing a reality detrimental to your sanity. Rejection is an evil spirit that must manifest. He must have a carrier. He must have a medium of expression. People who are manifesting Rejection are channeling a spirit of Rejection.

When a person is in bitterness, unforgiveness, resentment, retaliation, anger, wrath, hatred, violence, and murder, they are channeling these spirits within them. Rejection by others is a wound to the spirit.

The Power of Words

The words of a talebearer are as wounds, and they go down into the innermost parts of the belly. Proverbs 18:8

The words of a man's mouth are as deep waters. The words of a talebearer are as wounds. The impact of those words goes into the intellectual, emotional part of the soul and become part of our psyche. When someone rejects us, we hear their voice. It goes in our ears. Our brain processes it. The words coming from that other person were not the person speaking, but was an evil spirit speaking evil through them. There was a corresponding spirit on assignment that entered right into you to reinforce those words as part of your spiritual makeup forever. That is how it works.

Many people are into inner healing. I am not into inner healing. Those feelings and those emotions that you think in

your head and feel down in your belly are the presence of an
evil spirit, and it must be defeated. It can be defeated by
deliverance or when you stop agreeing with it. The Bible
says you are to know the truth; then the truth shall make
you free. The Spirit of God honors the Word of God.

> **And ye shall know the truth, and the truth shall make you**
> **free.** John 8:32

When the Word of God is spoken, evil spirits will leave
you. They are under the pressure of the anointing of the
Holy Spirit because the truth you are mixing with your faith
comes into your heart; their power is broken and they are
gone. We do not have to come around and stare into your
eyes for hours and say, "In the name of Jesus" a hundred
times for devils to leave. The entrance of the truth, which is
the Word of God, mixed with your faith can defeat every
evil spirit in your life.

That is why teaching is so important especially when
Scripture is read because that Scripture is life and power.
Jesus defeated the devil. He did not get deliverance. He just
quoted the Word. Entrance of truth can defeat the devil if it
is anointed by the Holy Spirit and mixed with your faith.
Truth is not intellectual. Truth is a Spirit. He is God, the
Word. Truth is a being, a spiritual being. People think truth
is just a philosophical idea. The Word of God is a spiritual
being. His name is Jesus.

Words can produce a wounding of the spirit, a broken
heart. The old saying "sticks and stones may break my
bones, but words will never hurt me" – what a lie that is.
Words have power. The Bible says in the tongue is life or
death. What you set into motion with your tongue is
honored, either by God or by Satan. The Bible says that
every word you say shall be held in judgment against you if

it is not dealt with under the blood and repented for, and there is no double jeopardy here. *You just have to get it right with God.*

There can be a lot of people standing there one day and the old tape recorder of heaven is going to play. Their words are going to stand in judgment against them. Every word that is spoken stands forever, and it either sends into motion the kingdom of God to execute it or the kingdom of the devil to execute it. There is no middle ground.

Words pierce to the very bottom of the heart. If you do not have Rejection, the words will not stay in you.

A Clean House

Consider what happens when you have been delivered of Rejection and someone comes along with an evil spirit. These spirits know exactly what they are doing, and they say these things to hurt you. You even feel hurt. You feel defilement from words. But because you are right with God and right with yourself and right with your neighbor and because you have spiritual understanding about that spirit that is trying to get into you, it does not stand a chance. There is no place for it. That is why you have to get it straight at this level.

The Bible says,

24When the unclean spirit is gone out of a man, he walketh through dry places, seeking rest; and finding none, he saith, I will return unto my house whence I came out.
25And when he cometh, he findeth it swept and garnished.

²⁶**Then goeth he, and taketh to him seven other spirits more wicked than himself; and they enter in, and dwell there: and the last state of that man is worse than the first.**

Luke 11:24-26

That evil spirit wants to come back. It does not mean it is going to come back looking for you every single day afterwards. There are enough evil people around you that have it that are going to dump on you anyway. When you have been delivered of Rejection, that critter comes on its little prowl back to your house and says, "Knock, knock, anybody home?"

To which you respond, "Who are you?"

It replies, "I am Rejection." Are you going to tell it to "Come on in," or are you filled up?

I am filled up with the knowledge of God, and I do not have that spirit within me anymore. Yet, when it comes knocking I FEEL it just as if it had never left. When it comes I FEEL its presence just as strongly as I felt it living in me for 30 years, because it comes by its nature and its feelings. When it comes, I have to make a decision. I have filled myself up with the knowledge of God and the Word of God. My eyes are wide open. I understand the battle. I understand what is in that person. That spirit is not coming to live in me anymore. I say,

> Sorry Rejection. No vacancy. You are not going to live in my life anymore. I am a child of God. I am not rejected. What is in that person is their evil. It is not mine.

When Satan came to Jesus, the Word says the devil found nothing in Him. No evil.

> **Hereafter I will not talk much with you: for the prince of this world cometh, and hath nothing in me.** John 14:30

You need to be filled up. Get filled up by loving God, loving yourself and loving your neighbor. If you will get to that place, the evil one cannot touch you because there is nothing within you it can hook up with.

Single Mindedness

There is a time when the devil is defeated, but you just cannot become complacent in that. You always have to keep your guard up. You are going to have to come to a place that, even if you have been delivered of Rejection and Bitterness and everything else, your enemy may not want to give you up too soon.

In Psalm 119:28 David is talking about his life.

> **My soul melteth for heaviness: strengthen thou me according unto thy word.** Psalm 119:28

David is dealing with a spirit of Heaviness. When you have Rejection in you, you feel heavy. If you are in your depressive state of Rejection, and I say to you, "Would you just raise your hands and praise the Lord for me please," then you are probably going to want to deck me because this thing feels so heavy.

David's soul melted because of heaviness, deep hurt, and depression out of Rejection. Rejection will produce heaviness, incredible feelings of hurt in your spirit, and depression. Rejection will affect your reasoning.

**You are preoccupied
with what hurt you.**

When you are in a state of Rejection, you are preoccupied with that heaviness, and you are preoccupied with your thoughts. Rejection will affect your emotions, and Rejection will affect your decision-making. Now we have a connection. The Bible says that the words went into the spirit, but now your soul and your thinking are being affected.

> **For as he thinketh in his heart, so is he: Eat and drink, saith he to thee; but his heart is not with thee.** Proverbs 23:7

Who you are spiritually is what you will be intellectually if you are honest with yourself. The soulish part is the expression of the spiritual existence. Your soul is a bridge between the spirit and the physical world.

Your soul is responding. That is why it says in Hebrews that the Word of God is quick and powerful, is able to separate the soul from the spirit, is able to separate your poor stinking thinking from your poor spiritual thinking so that you can get the entrance of truth into your spirit, which is life.

> **For the word of God is quick, and powerful, and sharper than any twoedged sword, piercing even to the dividing asunder of soul and spirit, and of the joints and marrow, and is a discerner of the thoughts and intents of the heart.**
> Hebrews 4:12

The washing of the water of the Word renews your mind. You are correct spiritually. Your thinking and your intellect now match your spirit, and you are now one with God in spirit and in soul. Your mind, your soul, and your spirit have become one in God and your thinking is no longer double minded.

Double Mindedness

A double minded man is unstable in all his ways.
James 1:8

A double minded man is unstable in all his ways. The biggest problem you have with Rejection is that it makes you double minded. **Double mindedness is the root for all insanity.** A double minded man is unstable in all his ways: that means in his thinking, in his spiritual thoughts, his soulish thoughts and his physical existence as a human being.

One day he is like this, the next day he is like that. One day he is up, one day he is down. One day he feels loved, one day he does not feel loved. One day he feels like he is a son or daughter of God, the next day he does not feel like he is a son or daughter of God. One day he is smiling, one day he is sad. One day he is jumping, one day he is stooping.

The Bible says to be single-minded, having the mind of Christ. We are to put on the mind of Christ, which is the Word of God, which is the very way God thinks.

Let this mind be in you, which was also in Christ Jesus:
Philippians 2:5

When we think like the devil and his kingdom, we are thinking in opposition to God's thinking. So one day we are over here thinking like the devil, the next day we are over here thinking like God. That is being double minded and that man is unstable in all his ways. Another scripture says: let not that man think - the double minded one - that he w ill receive anything from God.

> For let not that man think that he shall receive any thing of
> the Lord. James 1:7

So if one day you want to be loved and the next day you do not want to be loved, the next day you are in Rejection, you are not going to receive it. You are in torment. You are in a world of confusion.

You may not have known that Rejection can produce allergies. Rejection can also produce MCS/EI. It can produce a wide range of autoimmune problems because it includes fear. Rejection always includes fear as a component: Fear of man, Fear of rejection, Fear of failure, Fear of abandonment. Fear feeds into the principality of Rejection. Fear coupled with Rejection will destroy your health because it is a weight on your human spirit.

Your Inner Thoughts

Only God and the man know the thoughts of the man's own heart.

> For what man knoweth the things of a man, save the spirit
> of man which is in him? even so the things of God knoweth no
> man, but the Spirit of God. 1 Corinthians 2:11

There are many scriptures that indicate that God knows your thoughts. He knows your needs before you even ask Him.

In Rejection, you know your inner thoughts. You know what you are dealing with fifty percent of the time. The other fifty percent of the time you are stuffing it in denial. **What you stuff into denial is more of a torment than what you are thinking about** because it torments you in the very depth of your spiritual existence.

Rejection is a root of the tree. A tree has a root that many times is entangled with other roots. Rejection is not a single root of your life. Remember it is an open door for Bitterness. You cannot defeat Rejection if your heart has not been prepared before God to deal with Bitterness. If you do not know how to receive God's forgiveness, if you do not know how to forgive yourself, if you have not practiced forgiving others and walking in love, you cannot possibly defeat Rejection when it is there. It is impossible. If you have Envy and Jealousy, you cannot defeat Rejection either.

Separate Yourself from the Enemy

One of the key things in ministry is to start separating yourself from your evil and also start separating other people from their evil. It is about time the devil was found guilty. And it is about time we let the people off the hook.

Discernment

The deliverance for our Rejection is our acceptance by our husband, the Lord. Habakkuk says when you are reproved of the Lord you shall consider your answer to Him.

> **¹I will stand upon my watch, and set me upon the tower, and will watch to see what he will say unto me, and what I shall answer when I am reproved.**
> **²And the LORD answered me, and said, Write the vision, and make it plain upon tables, that he may run that readeth it.**
> Habakkuk 2:1-2

When you are reproved of the Lord and you are convicted and you make the change in your heart, that reproof of the Lord is not for condemnation. It is not Rejection. The chastening of the Lord or reproof of the

Lord is for your instruction, for your safety, for your provision. Habakkuk the prophet, speaking by the Spirit of God says, "Here is the deal. Now that you have been reproved and now that you have the picture and everything is cool, here is what you do. It is given to you as a vision for your direction. It is given to you as a vision for your future."

Discernment gives you vision. The lights go on and discernment gives you the ability to see. When you set out to drive to town, you are setting future tense into motion. Time is marching on. There are two dimensions that are involved in your life: time and distance. Your speed is a combination of time and distance: rate of time relative to distance. If you are driving at 60 miles an hour, you are going one mile for every minute. If you have 300 miles to drive and you average 60 miles an hour it is going to take you five hours. If you drive at 30 miles per hour for 300 miles, it is going to take you ten hours. And if you drive at 15 miles an hour, it is going to take you twenty hours.

Your future is your vision. Faith is the substance of things hoped for, the evidence is not yet seen (Hebrews 11:1). **Vision is your faith of the future.** God said, without a vision my people perish (Proverbs 29:19). Habakkuk said it this way: "When you have been reproved of the Lord and you are standing upon your tower, what will you say to Him?" Here is what you say to Him: "I got the picture Lord. I got the picture where I am going." That is the vision: where you are going.

You take the vision for your life that God has given you after you have been reproved (and your discernment is coming into focus), and you write the vision down. Habakkuk says to see the vision, write it down plainly on tablets. Write the vision down so, as you are running to execute your vision, you can refer to the vision that you have written down so that you can get where you are going, so that the vision may be fulfilled.

When the Holy Spirit comes and convicts you of Bitterness, of Envy and Jealousy, or of Rejection, you have to establish that God wants you delivered.

In dealing with Rejection, you have to make your vision. It has to exclude Rejection. Rejection does not need to tag along with you in your lifetime. It is detrimental to your sanity. It is detrimental to your health.

I have already established with you from the Word of God that there should be no reason spiritually why you should hang on to Rejection. First of all, the Lord is acquainted with it, and secondly, God has accepted you. He has removed from you the shame of your youth and has called you "His lovely wife." God loves you the way you are. He has a greater expectation for you and that is the vision.

The Armor of Rejection

Luke says,

> [20]But if I with the finger of God cast out devils, no doubt the kingdom of God is come upon you.
> [21]When a strong man armed keepeth his palace, his goods are in peace:
> [22]But when a stronger than he shall come upon him, and overcome him, he taketh from him all his armour wherein he trusted, and divideth his spoils.   Luke 11:20-22

Rejection is a strong man. He is armed and may be ruling your life. When Rejection armed keeps his palace, his goods are in peace. Rejection is in you. You are his house. When he is armed and has control of your life, his goods are in peace because he rules your life. However, God created *you* to be in charge of your destiny with Him because He created you for His pleasure.

Imagine the outline of a man with a line right down the middle of him. One side is shaded black and the other is white because that means purity and it contains all the things that are of God. The black side represents that which is not pure and contains all the things that are not of God. Even the parts that are in the black shaded area are actually part of your personality. When you need an attitude adjustment, there is something in your personality that is not of God. A person who comes around with continual Bitterness, Envy, Jealousy, Rejection, or Fear, is showing you their darker side.

Rejection is trusting in his armor. He is banking on the fact that he cannot be defeated, that he is going to live in your life and in your palace, and you are going to live down in the basement. He is going to live upstairs in the living room and eat your lunch. He will raid your refrigerator and live in peace while you are in torment. Rejection is torment.

When the evil spirit is manifesting through you, it is at peace. When the evil spirit is cast out, it wanders through a dry place looking for a place of rest. When it is cast out, it is now in torment and you are in peace. When the evil spirit is in you, he is in peace and you are in torment.

Good is the antidote for evil. The nine fruits of the Spirit are the antidotes for the fruits of the devil. Discernment and honesty will allow you to identify the enemies in your palace. Luke 11:22 says when one stronger than he shall come upon him and overcome him, he taketh from him all his armor wherein he trusted.

Rejection is trusting and banking on the fact that you have not forgiven. The armor to Rejection includes: Bitterness, Unforgiveness, Resentment, Retaliation, Anger and Wrath, Hatred, Violence, Murder, Envy and Jealousy, Fear, Fear of Rejection, Fear of abandonment, Fear of failure, Fear of man, Self-Accusation, Self-Hatred, Guilt, and lack of self-esteem. This is armor that the principality of Rejection is banking on to allow him to stay even if you identify him in your life.

There is an entanglement or web of the roots. **No evil spirit stands alone by itself**; it works in conjunction with other ones. That is the armor.

Say that you are over here dealing with Bitterness. You have received the Word of God with joy. As you are rejoicing and you are forgiving people, then Rejection pops up and says, "Well, let me remind you about so and so and what they did to you. Let's go ahead and replay this one. You do like reruns, don't you?" Over here Envy and Jealousy is saying, "You know they think they're charming, just kind of more perfect than you. Who do they think they are?" Then Fear is saying, "Well I don't know." All of a sudden you have the whole scenario flipping and flopping.

Roots

First Corinthians 2:11 says, "For what man knows the things of a man, save the spirit of man which is in him." If you are honest with yourself, you know what is inside you in your thinking. You know what your struggles are. You know what your fears are. You know where your thoughts are. If you try to put it out of your mind, those thoughts are going to come anyway. Thoughts come on you in spite of yourself! "I am not going to think about that again." It is hardly out of your mouth and there it is again – just tormenting you.

The hidden roots are things that we may not know. They may not be things that we know consciously or think about all the time. The roots to your problem may not be part of your conscious thinking. There may be even spirits of remembrance of disease; it may be a spirit of infirmity that wants to linger on. Your enemy, the devil, has programmed you in everything in your life. Evil spirits are invisible disembodied beings that live in the realm of the spirit and they are able to speak to you beyond the realm of conscious thought with impressions, feelings, thoughts and ideas. They are able to trigger things in your life without you even thinking about it.

When you say you are going to resist the devil, it means you are resisting his kingdom. Ephesians says,

> **For we wrestle not against flesh and blood, but against principalities, against powers, against the rulers of the darkness of this world, against spiritual wickedness in high places.** Ephesians 6:12

Behind the scenes there is an invisible web. Maybe you have pulled a small tree or a bush out of the ground. You have different size roots on the end of it. You have big roots, you have medium sized roots, you have little roots, and then you have the hair roots. A hair root looks just like a spider. All of these roots are tangled and webbed together, all of them drawing a source of water and nutrients from here to there. They feed into a common trunk to produce a common fruit, but they all work in conjunction with each other.

Behind the scenes in your life, you are the tree. There is either the manifestation of God or the devil is manifesting all over you, every single day. You are walking out. You are either a godly tree, an evil tree or you are half-and-half. Or you could be 30/70 or 40/60 or 65/35 or 90/10 – it is like an oil formula. As you go through your life, your thoughts, your words and your deeds, you are walking out and demonstrating one kingdom or the other. You are either the fruit of the devil or the fruit of God. God created you to be the fruit of Him.

In Genesis it says He created you in His own image. When the world sees us, we should be the image of God. Hidden roots are just that. They are beneath the surface. That is why the Bible says, "Only the spirit of man knows the thoughts of the man's heart." Only that tree knows what is underneath the ground. The only way you are going to know what is underneath your tree is to unearth it, uncover it, expose it, dig that tree up.

That is what is meant in Hebrews.

> **Neither is there any creature that is not manifest in his sight: but all things are naked and opened unto the eyes of him with whom we have to do.** Hebrews 4:13

He knows your roots. He knows what is in the ground of your life; it is no surprise to Him. You need to know your roots. You need to do an x-ray about what is underneath your trunk. There are things that we may not know consciously or think about all the time. I call this the beginning of understanding, the feeder system of what is feeding into who you are.

Rejection comes from this. Unforgiveness comes from this. Envy and jealousy comes from this. Fear comes from this. This feeder system entwines itself into our realities.

Many of the wounds that we receive in Rejection are hidden. The victim does not feel constantly rejected. You are not going around meditating on Rejection all the time, yet you are constantly, crucially affected by this power deep within. Rejection is always lurking, waiting for an opportunity to manifest in your life. You are not going around looking for ways to be rejected, but Rejection is looking for a way to manifest.

The Feeder System

The tangled system involves a feeder system. Let us identify the tangle.

1. False Responsibility

What is false responsibility? What is false burden bearing? What is false compassion? There are people who have Rejection that identify with the evil problems of others. **That what produces all support groups.** We call them massive pity parties. They gather around the problem instead of the solution. "Well, let me tell you about my bad day with fibromyalgia today." "Well, you think you had a bad day. Let me tell you about my bad day with fibromyalgia today." The first thing you know, you have 15 people over the next 3 hours talking about their bad day with fibromyalgia today.

No one would stand up and say, "Would anybody be interested in being free of fibromyalgia?" "Oh, God forbid! Get out of here. This is a very important meeting. We are here to discuss all the things that cause fibromyalgia. How dare you suggest there is a possibility of freedom? Do not touch our sacred cow."

False responsibility, false burden bearing, and false compassion are rooted in a companionship of Rejection.

Bearing one another's burdens does not mean that you bear the rotten roots like a beast of burden for the rest of your life. Bearing one another's burdens means you come along with this other person to take the burden off them; not help them carry it.

In ministry our job is to give you God and give you healing, not to come alongside you and create a massive support organization for your disease and help you shoulder your burden through life. That is not burden bearing. That is false burden bearing.

Self-pity comes along and says, "You do not understand me. If you loved me and you are a good Christian like you are supposed to be, you would help me carry this problem." "Well, how many years would you suggest I do it?"

Rejection has a lot of tangled things to it.

2. Fear of Deliverance

Many people are afraid to be free because deliverance can produce a drastic personality change. Some people are afraid of what they will be like when they are free. They are afraid to think, "Well how will I think, how will I act? What will I be like? I do not know if I want to change. I have been this way for forty years. I do not know if I could stand not having Rejection as part of my life. Bitterness, Envy, Jealousy, Rejection and Fear have been a part of me for so long, I cannot fathom not having this as part of my thinking. I do not think I want to be free." This may sound strange but they tell me that a prisoner that is sentenced to life becomes so uncomfortable when he is set free that he wants to go back to prison. He does not want to be free. He does not know how to live in freedom.

Maybe you are so accustomed to Rejection, Bitterness, Envy, Jealousy, and Fear that the thought of being free intrigues you, but you are just not committed to freedom. I have met people who do not want to be well. First of all, they might lose some things they like. If you are well, you are capable of going back into life and working. If you are well, you do not have to be taken care of anymore.

Sometimes people have been so rejected from childhood that the disease is the first time in their life they have had any attention given to them. At least they are important now. At least when someone comes around they say, "Oh, how are you feeling today?" Oh, someone noticed.

Rejection is a place of identity. Deliverance will remove your evil disease identity.

3. Fear of Being Vulnerable

Many people need the spiritual handicap of Rejection as a defense mechanism of protection. Rejection is an easy place to run to. One of the biggest areas in MCS/EI is that a person does not want to take the risk of being rejected ever again. They decide, "I am just not going to be vulnerable." When you have made up your mind that you are not going to be vulnerable, you create a whole labyrinth of defense mechanisms to protect you from Rejection. No wonder you are worn out.

One of the great things that has happened in the healing of MCS/EI is that the people who have been totally healed are no longer afraid of being rejected and they do not mind being vulnerable. They can be hurt by someone's words, and it just does not affect them any more.

Here's something to think about:

**About 60 to 70 percent
of all Rejection is imagined.**

4. Feeling Unloved

This can be real or imagined. A personality of Rejection will make you feel rejected even when you are not rejected. It will create scenarios within your mind. The sights, sounds, voices, faces, scenarios, flashbacks, and projections cause you to imagine yourself rejected even when you are not. You just listened to a lie and believed it.

5. Dissatisfaction

Discontent is like a drop of water dancing on the top of a hot stove – never satisfied; always looking around, always comparing yourself with others, always dissatisfied.

Being discontent affects your appearance, how you talk, how you look, your job, your marriage. You may even church hop. You lack satisfaction and you are not happy in relationships.

Malcontent and being discontent with everything in life is a product of Rejection. Just as untreated and neglected *physical* wounds may fester and grow worse and create massive problems, so do *spiritual* and *emotional* wounds. If unattended, they will fester and grow into spiritual gangrene. If you discern a spiritual problem in you and you do not deal with it, it will not just go away some day. It will fester and spread. It is also contagious.

This is what the Word says about sin, and it says it very bluntly: die to it! The second part is this: take the spiritual sword of God, which is the Word of God, and carve the sin out of your life.

Sin destroys like a cancer. What do they do with cancer? Take a surgeon's knife and cut out the cancer to keep it from infecting the rest of the body and destroying the whole body.

Jesus said, "If you have two hands and one hand is dabbling over in the evil side, cut that hand off because it would be best for you to go into heaven with one hand than go into hell with two. If you have an eye that sees evil along with your good eye, it would be best for you to pluck your eye out and go into heaven with one eye than go into hell with two eyes. If you have two feet, one takes you to evil, one takes you to good, it would be best to cut that leg off and go into heaven with one leg, than to go into hell with two" (Matthew 5:29-30).

6. Not Being Nurtured

People were supposed to nurture you and love you, but they did not. That could have been your mother, father, grandmother, grandfather, boss, brother, sister, husband, or wife. They are negligent, they are indifferent, and they do not consider your presence or you as being valuable. A tremendous feeder into Rejection is being around those who just consider you a non-person.

7. Rejection in the Womb

Other feeders are Rejection at conception, in the womb, unwanted pregnancy and illegitimacy.

8. Resentment about Birth

Resentment by the parent about the birth of a child because of economic problems feeds Rejection. They resent the financial burden they feel the child represents.

9. Marital Problems of Parent

Another feeder root into this web is marital problems of the parents.

10. Personal Marital Problems

Personal marital problems of the adult feeds Rejection. It could be your parents' marital problems or it could be your marital problems. Whenever you have marital problems, you have Rejection. **Marital problems always involve Rejection.**

Solutions for Identity Crisis

We have three classes of Rejection: Rejection by God, Self-Rejection and Rejection by others.

Did you know that you can reject yourself? God could accept you, others could accept you, yet you look at yourself and say you are unacceptable.

If Rejection came by adoption, freedom from Rejection comes from adoption. What a paradox. Instead of being abandoned in adoption, we are now accepted in adoption and restored to God that we can say Abba Father.

The identity solution is to know who you are in Christ and who you are in the Father. Romans 8:15 says you have not been given the spirit of bondage again to fear, but of adoption whereby you can cry out Abba Father.

The next thing as an identity solution: you do not have to strive to have an identity. Your Father in heaven will bring it to pass in your life.

Know Who You Are in Christ

Knowing who you are in Christ is of prime importance. This is the antidote to an identity crisis. Acceptance is the antidote to Rejection. The Father has accepted you, but have you accepted yourself?

Rejection will not allow you to accept yourself. Self-Rejection, Self-Hatred, Guilt, Unloving spirits, images, impressions and emotions will tell you that you are not the "fairest of them all."

Jesus dealt with that in Isaiah 53. It said very clearly that He was not a man that you would desire Him after the flesh. He was not comely, and there was nothing in physical appearance that would appeal to you.

> **For he shall grow up before him as a tender plant, and as a root out of a dry ground: he hath no form nor comeliness; and when we shall see him, there is no beauty that we should desire him.** Isaiah 53:2

If you saw Jesus as a man you probably would be offended. You would say, "Well, I want a handsome man to follow. I want someone 6 feet 5 inches. They have to look very much perfect." If you are following someone because of the way they look, you have an identity crisis and you have Rejection. You are looking for a role model after the flesh. Paul said to know no man after the flesh. That is why the fruits of the Holy Spirit in Galatians 5 have nothing to do with your physical body. It has to do with your nature, which is who you are on the inside. As a man thinks in his heart, so is he (Proverbs 23:7).

An Heir of the Father

Galatians says,

> Now I say, That the heir, as long as he is a child, differeth nothing from a servant, though he be lord of all;   Galatians 4:1

There are four components in this verse about your identity in the Father:

First, you are an heir.

Second, you are a child.

Third, you are a servant.

Fourth, you are lord of all.

When it says you are an heir that does not mean you have inherited anything. If you have inherited everything, that would not make you an heir. Do you have an identity crisis because you have not partaken of your inheritance? You may try to create your own inheritance because you cannot wait. You may try to be a lord before your time. That may be your identity problem.

Rejection will not let you be content at the level that God has you. If you are all stirred up all the time and are stewing in your juices because everything is bothering you and nothing is going right, then you have Rejection. Someone should have done it this way or they should have done it that way. This is wrong or that is wrong. Life is just not going the way you think it should go. These are the fruits of Rejection. **Rejection will never allow you to be content.**

The Word says: In all things give thanks for this is the will of God.

In every thing give thanks: for this is the will of God in Christ Jesus concerning you. 1 Thessalonians 5:18

Rejection will not allow you to give thanks because Rejection is never content. When you do not have an identity, you are not content. You are dressing yourself up (and there is nothing wrong with looking good). There is nothing wrong with new clothing. But there is something wrong with looking nice and getting dressed up if you are doing it to satisfy Rejection or Self-Rejection. You are trying to elevate the serotonin levels coming out of unloveliness, Self-Rejection, Self-Hatred, Guilt, Fear of Rejection, Fear of abandonment.

Galatians 4:1 says, "Now I say, that the heir as long as he is a child differeth nothing from a servant, though he be lord of all." Paul is saying that your identity of the future has nothing to do with your present state. Rejection will always project into the future an unfulfilled reality concerning your identity and your position.

I solved this scripturally in my heart from the Word of God a long time ago as an individual. I learned it from poor Mr. Nebuchadnezzar when he ended up eating grass like an animal for seven years. He had a powerful statement when he came back to his sanity. He said, "I know this: that it is God that sets up and it is God that sets down." That means it is God that establishes men for His purposes. It is God that does it.

The solution for your identity crisis is to let God take control. There are certain things that we do, or do not do, and there are things that we are required to do. You must settle something in your heart. If you will submit to God in your life, if you will draw nigh to God, if you will seek God, if you will deal with the junk in your life, you will be everything that God planned for you to be from the foundation of the world. You will not have to do anything about it. You just have to show up with a right spirit submitting yourself to God and allowing the Holy Spirit access to your life, to lead you. The scriptures say,

> For as many as are led by the Spirit of God, they are the sons of God. Romans 8:14

Rejection will not allow you to be led. Rejection will drive you into a solution for identity, or it will keep you from your identity, which is another phase of Rejection.

Rejection can keep you from your identity or it will drive you into one; the wrong one. So you have two sides to this coin. Rejection will keep you from your identity or it will drive you into a fabricated identity.

You may not yet have arrived in who you think you should be as a man or a woman. Do not worry about it. You do not have to have a problem with Rejection. God the Father has appointed you for your season. Do not worry about what you are going to do in this life. Submit to God and He will have His way in your life.

When you say, "Abba Father," Rejection should be broken forever because when you say, "Abba Father," you are saying, "My Father." He is saying to you, "My son and My daughter."

No more identity crisis and no more Rejection because in spite of Bitterness, in spite of the failure of your generations, in spite of your mother and father, in spite of your failure, in spite of everything, the spirit of adoption is here and the spirit of adoption breaks Rejection.

No Striving to Have Identity.

Another part of the identity solution is not only knowing who you are in Christ, not only recognizing that you have not been given the spirit of bondage again to fear, but that you do not have to strive to have an identity.

God has already determined your identity, and He will bring it to pass if you will let Him by faith. He has already determined your identity. If you try to create your own identity, it will be out of Rejection and Fear. The way to get God into your life so that your identity can be established is to get Fear and Rejection out of your life. Thereby you no longer will be driven, but you will be led.

Fear and Rejection drive you, but adoption leads you. My children are in no hurry to get on with life. They are busy following their father in their life until the stage comes where they are on their own. They do not worry about where the next meal is coming from. They do not worry about whether they have clothing to wear. They do not worry about how much money they are making in their job. They do not need a job. Everything is being provided for them within the parameters of what their welfare needs.

You, as sons and daughters of God, can enjoy the same privileges: you can enjoy a place to live. You can enjoy food for your tummies. You can enjoy clothing on your back. It is an automatic provision by God for you. If you will accept your sonship and if you will take your place in the family of God without Fear and without Rejection, then you might be surprised what God can do for you. If you reject God as your

Father, if you reject His provision, you may find yourself in some difficulty in your life.

Reversing Rejection

How do you reverse Rejection? The reversal of Rejection is accepting God's love and acceptance without exception.

Get Rid of Self-Rejection.

You have to get rid of Self-Rejection. If God be for you, who could be against you? You have no right to reject yourself if God has accepted you. When you do, you make God a liar. You say: "God, You made a mistake when You created me. I am rejected and for You to tell me that I am not rejected is a lie. So You are a liar." When you go into Self-Rejection, you are telling Him He is a liar.

You need to repent for not being honest with Him about your heart. He has accepted you through Jesus Christ. For God so loved the world that He gave His only begotten Son.

> For God so loved the world, that he gave his only begotten Son, that whosoever believeth in him should not perish, but have everlasting life.　　　　　　　　　　John 3:16

Ezekiel 18:32. It is not **Adonay Yehovih's** will that any man should perish, but all should live and not die.

> For I have no pleasure in the death of him that dieth, saith the Lord God: wherefore turn yourselves, and live ye.
> 　　　　　　　　　　　　　　　　　　Ezekiel 18:32

Not Letting Other's Rejection of You Get to You.

If someone has Rejection themselves, they are going to reject you.

Whatever spiritual problem a person has must manifest at some point. If they have Bitterness, it is going to come up at some point. If they have Envy and Jealousy, it is going to come up at some point. If they have Rejection, it is going to come up at some point.

Paul said in Romans 2 that what you accuse another of and at the same time excuse yourself of, you yourself are.

> Therefore thou art inexcusable, O man, whosoever thou art that judgest: for wherein thou judgest another, thou condemnest thyself; for thou that judgest doest the same things.   Romans 2:1

Fear Feeds Rejection

Second Timothy says,

> For God hath not given us the spirit of fear; but of power, and of love, and of a sound mind.   2 Timothy 1:7

The antidote for Fear is the Godhead. Love is the Father. The sound mind is the Word of God, who is Jesus. Power is the Holy Ghost. So the antidote for Fear is the Father, the Word, who is the Son, and the Holy Ghost. Fellowship with the Godhead drives fear away every day.

You need to start every day with fellowship with God. If you wake up in the morning stewing in your juices about what can go wrong that day, you are not fellowshipping with the Godhead, you are fellowshipping with the devil.

If you get up and the first thing you do in the morning is plan your strategy around Fear for the rest of that day, you are having breakfast with the devil and that will become the focus of your day. What you are going to avoid, what you are not going to avoid, who you are going to avoid. What you are going to eat, what you are not going to eat, where you are going to drive, where you are not going to drive. Your whole day is spent projecting the failure of something.

Sources of Rejection

Let's look at some possible sources of rejection.

The number one source of rejection is children growing up without a father. This produces a lack of identity or even no identity. The bastard's curse carries down 10 generations according to the Law. Aren't you glad that through Jesus it can be broken in your generation? Aren't you glad the law was fulfilled in Christ so that you can appropriate those things to your life and be free?

Another possible source of rejection is growing up without a father. The father establishes the identity and the emotional stability of a child, especially in a female. That is why, in my home, females get away with everything and the boys do not. They really get ticked off. "Dad, these girls get away with everything." Well, they don't really. But there is a place of provision and safety for the females in my home that the guys wish they had because I teach the boys that they are going to have to look out for the females.

You cannot possibly be a husband one day if you do not get this under control. If you do not respect your sister, you will never respect your wife. If you do not respect your mother, you will never respect your wife. If you touch my wife, you touch me and you're in trouble. Because if you touch my wife with your mouth, you touch me because we are one flesh. You will have a bigger problem than you ever thought.

Ask my children if they can sass their mother. Ask them how far they are going get without respecting the law of the mother. Not very far...why? Because the safety of the female must be established. Once it is established, she will be whole in the family because her identity comes from the man, and the man's identity comes from God. I do not know whether you like that or do not like it, it's the godly order. Now, because it's been perverted in mankind because of sin, it's not God's problem, and it's not my problem. So do not judge me on that statement about the base of the perversion of men because of sin. It is still the godly order.

The Bible says the head of the woman is the man. The head of man is Christ. That is what it says in Scripture. I didn't make anything up. I just quoted it to you because it's been perverted. Because certain females have been victimized by an ungodly man does not change the precept. You do not change the precept; you change the man who's perverting it.

Bring this into your heart. I suppose that is why God raised up a guy like me, with 90 percent of his caseload being female, because it takes someone to get them healed. Now a lot of females have a problem with me because I'm a little intense, but that intensity is a warring for freedom not insensitivity. I do not like your enemy but I care for you a lot.

Not Having a Father in the Home

Rejection comes from not having a father in the home. Forty percent of black families in America do not have a man at home, whether a married man or an unmarried. Twenty-five percent of all families do not have a man at home. Rejection is a big enemy. No father, no godly father image, produces lack of identity. No father in the home is a source of Rejection

Many, many, many females go into promiscuity and pornography themselves because of a need to be loved by a man. All adultery, fornication, and sexual contact outside of marriage is driven by the need to be loved. All sexual addictions are rooted in the need to be loved because of rejection. Because of rejection! Males go into promiscuity and pornography for the same reason.

Now you know why we have to get rid of rejection! If rejection isn't around, guess how you're going to feel? Loved and accepted. Is that a fair exchange? Do you want to feel loved and accepted? I do. What robs you of that? Rejection.

I have been around for a while as a husband and a father. It is amazing how the children, in a godly setting, usually obey a father faster than they will obey a mother. Have you noticed that? That is why a family without a father at home produces a mother who is a victim of the children. It is not always true, but many times she struggles with obedience because kids just will not obey their mother.

When I have ever seen sass and derogatory statements from a child, it has been directed at the mother before it is ever directed toward the father. Why is that? Because there is a respect for the father that is built into that situation in spite of rebellion. That is a godly reality. Now I have seen boys spout out at their father. I have seen daughters spout at their father, and if that is the case, it is because the father did not earn their respect.

Sometimes a father is in the home, yet the wife and the children do not respect him because he does not show godly mannerism. So what would be one of the criteria for getting free of rejection in this situation? You have to be able to respect someone. If you do not respect someone, that is a tough issue, isn't it?

If we want to reverse this, we have to have a roll model, but establishing a role model is almost impossible because of perversion. There has to be a point of reference here somewhere.

Deliverance

There are only three deliverance prerequisites for being free of Rejection.

Accept God's Love

The prerequisite for being free of Rejection is to accept God's love. You do not just accept God's love, but you come forth and express it to Him and say,

> Father, thank you for adopting me. I recognize that my ancestors turned away from you and made the devil their father. I acknowledge that. I take responsibility for that and I ask to be free from that great tragedy of making the devil our spiritual father. I accept my forgiveness. I come before You, Father, and I accept Your love.
>
> You said that You loved us in John 3:16. John said in 1 John 3 that You are love. Paul said in Galatians 5 that one of the fruits of the Holy Spirit is love. You said in Your Word that You have not given us a spirit of fear, but power and love.

Father, take away my Rejection. Take away the spirit of Rejection from my life that keeps me from accepting Your love, Father. And give me the ability to accept You unconditionally and Your love for me by faith because You said it. You are not a man that You should lie, nor the son of man that You should repent. But You are truth, Father, and I believe You love me. Lord, You came to show us the Father. Please give me the ability and the freedom to love my Father in heaven."

Again, the first prerequisite for freedom from Rejection is a relationship with God the Father, cultivated by faith. Do not judge Him on the basis of the evil fathers you might have had in your life. He is not guilty by association just because the word *father* is attached to His name.

We could say this: Hitler was a man. Hitler was evil. Hitler was an evil man, therefore all men are evil. That is not a true statement. The math does not match. Even though the ingredients are there, it does not match. God is not evil just because men are. God the Father has not rejected you, even though other men have. He is not guilty. He is called the Father of all spirits. Those who worship Him must worship Him in Spirit and in truth.

> **God is a Spirit: and they that worship him must worship him in spirit and in truth.**   John 4:24

Rejection is not accepting God's love. It does not negate God's acceptance. If you reject God's love, it does not make God a liar. It only makes you guilty of not accepting something that has been given freely to you.

A prerequisite for deliverance would be a love for God and acceptance by Him. Relationships slowly develop over a period of time. Cultivate that conversation with God by faith; talk to Him.

When you talk to Him, believe that He heard you because if you doubt in your heart that He has heard you, you have wasted your time praying. If you are just praying hoping that He will listen to your voice floating through space somewhere, forget it. That is not in faith. That is like scattering your voice to the wind. Be specific. Come before His throne boldly in the name of the Lord Jesus and tell Him. Let your requests and your petitions be made known before God day in and day out but do not make Him a slot machine.

Get into a relationship with the Father. Your enemy, the devil, will use Bitterness, Rejection, Envy and Jealousy to keep you from the Father because **when you are preoccupied with this junk you will not even think about Him**. When you are busy thinking about your enemy and how he is evil to you, you are not in conversation with God because you cannot say and think two different things at the same time.

Love Yourself

The second prerequisite in deliverance from Rejection is that you must love and accept yourself. It does not mean that you get stuck on yourself. That would be another problem. You must accept yourself. You must accept yourself just as you are.

Love Your Neighbor

The third prerequisite is that you must love your neighbor as you love yourself. You cannot love your neighbor if you do not love yourself. You would be full of envy and jealousy. It is impossible for you to love your neighbor if you do not love yourself. It is impossible to love yourself if you have not received the love of God. It is just not possible.

So the prerequisites for freedom from Rejection are:

- Making peace with God once and for all.

- Making peace with yourself once and for all.

- Making peace with your brother once and for all (even if it is 70 times 7 in your relationship of forgiveness)

Love

First Corinthians 13 is probably the best part of the Bible you know and do not live by.

> ¹Though I speak with the tongues of men and of angels, and have not charity, I am become as sounding brass, or a tinkling cymbal.
> ²And though I have the gift of prophecy, and understand all mysteries, and all knowledge; and though I have all faith, so that I could remove mountains, and have not charity, I am nothing.
> ³And though I bestow all my goods to feed the poor, and though I give my body to be burned, and have not charity, it profiteth me nothing.
> ⁴Charity suffereth long, and is kind; charity envieth not; charity vaunteth not itself, is not puffed up, 1 Corinthians 13:1-4

Being mean is retaliation. Longsuffering is the opposite of resentment. Love is kind. Anger, wrath and hatred are the opposite of kindness. Charity envieth not. It is not jealous. It is not covetous. Love does not look around and study others, comparing itself to them. Charity vaunteth not itself nor puffs up itself. Love does not exalt itself over another.

You are to prefer your neighbor over or above yourself. The Scriptures say you are to defer one to another. There needs to be some yield signs.

> **⁵Doth not behave itself unseemly, seeketh not her own, is not easily provoked, thinketh no evil;**
> **⁶Rejoiceth not in iniquity, but rejoiceth in the truth;**
> **⁷Beareth all things, believeth all things, hopeth all things, endureth all things.** 1 Corinthians 13:5-7

Think no evil. Rejoice not in iniquity, but rejoice in the truth. Bear all things. Believe all things. Hope all things. Endure all things. That is love.

If anybody fails in any of these areas, you get your little sheet out and you remember it for a long time. It is amazing that we regard the failures of others, but we do not keep a rap sheet on ourselves.

If you are not prepared to receive God's love, if you are not prepared to accept yourself, if you are not prepared to love your neighbor as yourself, you will never be free from Rejection. It is not possible to be free if you do not accept God's love and yourself in it. It is not possible to be free if you do not accept yourself, and if you do not accept others as the attitude of your heart.

False love

Rejection will want to give you false love. If you want people just to speak good things about you to appease Rejection that is not a solution since your peace depends on someone else being nice. Your freedom from Rejection does not depend on another person liking you or saying good things about you, or smiling at you, or doing anything good for you. Your freedom from Rejection comes from you, positionally, knowing your identity regardless of any other person.

You know what Jesus said in Matthew 26.

> **And he went a little farther, and fell on his face, and prayed, saying, O my Father, if it be possible, let this cup pass from me: nevertheless not as I will, but as thou wilt.**
> Matthew 26:39

That was His moment of human weakness, but then He snapped right around. He said if it be possible take this cup from Me, but nevertheless Thy will be done, not Mine.

Without real love, you will have a false love that is counterfeit and subject to the whims of approval by others. If who you are depends on someone else's approval, then that is a false love. The Bible says that love covers a multitude of sins. If we have real love, I am going to love you whether you are good or whether you are bad, whether you do right things or whether you do bad things. My relationship with you does not depend on my approval of you. It depends on our relationship together because we are sons and daughters of God.

If you perceive love to be someone's approval of you, then you are on shaky ground because that is false love. Remember the expression "fair weather friends?" Your friends are those who are there when the storms blow, when you have lost everything.

Who you are and who you are in love is not dependent on the approval of another. You should feel as safe in failure as you do in success. Jesus struggled, but He felt as safe in failure from a natural sense as He did in success. Are you willing to lay your life down at that level? If you do, Rejection can never touch you.

Fear not what man can do unto you.

> **In God have I put my trust: I will not be afraid what man can do unto me.** Psalm 56:11

Prevention of Disease

When the curse is broken in ministry, we do not have to go back and undo the generations behind it that caused it. We have to begin right where we need to begin, and that is where it gets broken. When it gets broken there, that component will not be there for the generations that are coming in the future.

That is why in ministry, if pastors really want to get serious about serving God, they need to sit down with their people, look at the history, the spiritual history, and the disease history of that family. Then, before God break this stuff off so that the children that are going to be born will not be born with the inherited curse. If we will do that, we will have done something very significant.

That beats healing of disease. That is **prevention of disease**. I believe as a minister, and I hope to achieve this in my generation, we are going to start teaching the ingredients of disease *prevention*, not just healing. I believe that one of the provisions of the atonement because of knowledge, is that we can break curses in family trees and in people before they ever get married. When they do get married it can be broken before there is ever a conception. When that child is born, we will not have to deal with many of the diseases that that child would have to deal with as a child or as an adult. It just will not be there. That is my goal. If we can do that, we have done something very significant.

Exodus says,

> [5]...visiting the iniquity of the fathers upon the children unto the third and fourth generation of them that hate me;
> [6]And shewing mercy unto thousands of them that love me, and keep my commandments.   Exodus 20:5-6

As a minister I want to break the curse of the third and fourth generations, and I want to establish blessing to a thousand generations. If you wait for mommy and daddy to get it together, you are going to be here for a long time. Maybe if mommy and daddy see you get free, they might come looking for themselves, and then you can explain to them how you gained freedom from the curses that they have. Maybe they will get saved and get free too. That is reversing the curse. From a standpoint of intercession, what you can do is set the process in motion for God to deal with their hearts to bring them into a place where He can set them free.

You cannot break curses over someone else without their permission. The curse can only be broken over those who are obedient to God and keep His commandments. You must be born again.

Now I have seen God heal people who were sinners. I have seen Him deliver people who did not qualify. And when they were healed and delivered, they followed God. He said I shall have mercy on whom I shall have mercy.

> For he saith to Moses, I will have mercy on whom I will have mercy, and I will have compassion on whom I will have compassion.   Romans 9:15

Spiritual roots and spiritual blocks are important. God's sovereignty of love and provision is incredibly powerful. We always have to be open to the possibility that God will do a quick work.

When you start praying for your family or your family tree, I believe that sets into motion many, many things of God to bring things to come to pass. **Do not look at it from the basis of the curse that needs to be broken. Look at it from the basis of God's love for them that needs to be put into motion.** I believe that when you start praying for others, those prayers move the hand of God. I see a powerful provision for us executing the will of God.

My definition of prayer is "executing the known will of God." Ezekiel 18 defines the known will of God, "It is not God's will that any man should perish." If it is not God's will that any man should perish, then what kind of prayer should you pray? **You pray for their freedom and their salvation.**

I believe it from Isaiah.

> Thus saith the Lord, the Holy One of Israel, and his Maker, Ask me of things to come concerning my sons, and concerning the work of my hands command ye me.   Isaiah 45:11

Isaiah says, "Ask me of things to come concerning my sons." A person who is not born again is not a son yet. Intercession is just a prayer on behalf of someone else who is not praying for himself. If you are not saved, you cannot pray for yourself. You do not have any sense about it. It takes someone who has some sense about it. We come before the Father and say,

> Father, I see in Your Word that it is not Your will that any man should perish or die, but all should live and come to salvation. On behalf of Johnny or Sally, I ask you to watch over Your Word and go after them.

The beginning of breaking the curse in a family tree is sending God to them out of your love.

Curses in Children

What about breaking the curse over a child before the years of understanding? The Bible says the child is sanctified by the believing parent (1 Corinthians 7:14). There is a provision for children who are not at the years of understanding. I have seen it happen where children have been delivered of diseases when the curse is broken in the parent. I have seen children automatically healed when a parent was delivered. I believe it can happen just like that. When that curse is broken, it sets them free because that child is sanctified by the believing parent. If the parent is a believer and the curse is broken, I do not see any reason at all why that minor child shouldn't be set free at the same time.

A child can go back to Isaiah 45 and set in motion prayers concerning his ancestry. When the children of the captivity realized why their parents had been in captivity, they confessed their sins and the sins of their fathers (Nehemiah 9:2). I believe a child can pray for his unsaved parent regardless of how old the child is. Prayer changes things. Is the parent sanctified by the believing child? No, there is no scripture to back it.

However, James 5:16 says the effectual fervent prayer of a righteous man avails much. If I were a child, I would pray for my parents. If I were a parent, I would pray for my children, and I would ask God to go after them. I believe there is power in that type of prayer.

You may say, "Well, I have not seen it happen yet." I want to tell you something. I was a prodigal; I wasted 38 years of my life. I was dedicated to God. I was born out of death. There was a Hannah-type covenant made concerning me in my life, in the very throes of death as my mother was dying from cancer. My mother was healed and lived 33 more years. She died in faith concerning me. It was seven years after she died before I came to the Lord. I believe her prayers were thundering in the ears of God and demanding my freedom from Satan. In my day, seven years later, I came back to God, and I have been here ever since.

Do not stop praying. Do not go into unbelief and doubt because in my case, my mother died in the faith never having seen the object of her faith. But here I am today. You know what it says about Abraham – he died in the faith never having seen the fruit of it in his lifetime.

Whatsoever You Loose on Earth...

Your freedom does not depend on the resolution with any other person on the face of this earth. It depends on your resolution before God personally first.

The Word says those sins that you retain are retained, those sins you release are released.

> And I will give unto thee the keys of the kingdom of heaven: and whatsoever thou shalt bind on earth shall be bound in heaven: and whatsoever thou shalt loose on earth shall be loosed in heaven. Matthew 16:19

When you retain another's sins, you retain it over yourself and you retain it over them. Many people may end up in hell some day because someone would not forgive them. It binds them to a curse. **When you do not forgive someone, you are binding them to a curse**. But you are also bringing the same curse back on your own head. If you are binding unforgiveness in the earth, it is bound in heaven. If you loose unforgiveness in the earth, it is loosed in heaven. If you retain sins in the earth, they are retained. If you loose them, they are loosed.

This is a vicious war. And there are no winners in unforgiveness. There are no winners in Rejection, and there are no winners in Envy and Jealousy. There are no winners and there are no survivors. It is death. Unforgiveness is murder. Envy and Jealousy produces death. Rejection produces death.

Jesus said on the cross: Father, forgive them for they know not what they do. Stephen said, when he was dying after being stoned, "Father, forgive them. They know not what they do." What are you supposed to do? You too can say, "Father, forgive them, they know not what they do." Be aware, a voice may say to you, "Yes, they knew better than that." No, they did not; they were possessed with Bitterness and Rejection themselves just like you are, but not for long. Rejection has to go. Bitterness has to go.

Repentance

If you are ready to repent, this prayer of repentance may help you:

> Father, I repent to You for listening to a lie from a lying man accusing me and telling me I was rejected, or a lying spirit that would have accused me to myself, telling me I was rejected. When I listen to that, I have made man my god and I have made You, Father, a liar. I repent to You, Father, for allowing Rejection to rule my life. I repent to You, Father, for turning away from Your love, not accepting it unconditionally.
>
> I repent for my Fear of man.
>
> I repent for my Fear of failure.
>
> I repent for my Fear of rejection.
>
> I repent for my Fear of abandonment.
>
> I repent for my unbelief and my doubt.
>
> I repent for my faithlessness.
>
> I repent for my ignorance.
>
> I repent for the sins of my ancestry that followed this course and then brought it into my life. I ask You to forgive them. I acknowledge their transgressions, and I acknowledge it in my own life. I repent to You, Father.

I accept Your love according to the Word of God. I mix it with my faith. I accept You, Father, as my heavenly Father once and for all through Jesus Christ. I am not rejected. My inheritance is a son or daughter of God, a finished product now, by faith. I am your son or your daughter.

I accept You, Father, as You have accepted me. I settle this once and for all in my heart. My family may have been full of Rejection, but I do not have to be a carrier in my generation any longer. I do not have to be a carrier of the spiritual parasite called Rejection.

Rejection, I know you. I see you. I understand what you have done to my family tree. I know what you have done to me. I am not in agreement with you. You are not going to rule my life. You are a lying spirit. Let God be true and let you be a liar. Amen.

Overcome the Enemy

That confession will be a declaration of your heart and it will be a declaration to establish you in your acceptance. The opposite of Rejection is acceptance.

Look at what parasites do in certain diseases. When the immune system is strengthened and is again strong, a parasite does not stand a chance because the white cells attack it and destroy it as an outside invader. When you have arrived in your heart by faith and your spirit man has made his peace with God in acceptance, those spiritual parasites never stand a chance either. When the enemy comes in like a flood, the Spirit of God through you shall raise a standard against the enemy (Isaiah 59:19).

How do you participate with God? By resisting the devil, and drawing nigh to God. He'll draw nigh to you. Mix what you have heard with faith. Make it part of your spiritual life and let your poor minds be renewed by the washing of the water of the Word and establish new memes. Establish new units of memory that project into the future exactly what God has said about you. You are not rejected. You are accepted.

This is the age, not of judgment, not of the law, but of grace and of mercy. Grace and mercy says you are accepted. Grace is unmerited favor, and mercy says you are not guilty even though your enemy says you are guilty. God says you are not guilty by faith. You are receiving His favor regardless of those things that you have not grown out of in your spiritual life.

You can come boldly before the throne of grace. You do not have to come in before the Father with your head hanging down. Many denominations teach that you are a worm not worthy to receive. That violates the scripture that says you are to boldly come before the throne of grace. The Lord said: I no longer call you servants, I call you friends. So there are these people going around, "Well, I am just a worm. I am not worthy to receive His blessings. I am not worthy, so I will come before the Father with my head hanging down and say here, Father, here is your worm. Bless your worm."

The only time I find the word worm in Scripture is a literal worm that ate the body of Herod because he considered himself a god. The other time was the life essence of the damned that lived forever in the lake of fire. That can be found in Isaiah 66 and also in Mark 9, "Where their worm dieth not." That word *worm* literally means the life essence; the spirit essence of the person. It does not mean that you are a worm.

Discernment

Firstly, spiritual roots must be identified and revealed by you and the Holy Spirit or someone that has accurate spiritual discernment. You must x-ray your spiritual life. You say, "But Pastor, it hurts, I do not like what I see." Alright, so you have a fever, and it will not go away. Ignore it. When you go to the doctor, what are you looking for? A diagnosis of the problem. When you come to the pastor about something in your life, what are you looking for? A diagnosis of the problem. When you go to the doctor and he gives you the diagnosis, **you have a choice to make: either deal with it, or walk out and say I do not want to deal with it.** Saying you do not want to deal with it does not make the problem go away.

If you kept going back to the doctor and every day you are knocking at his door saying, "Doctor, I am sick today."

"I gave you the diagnosis yesterday. I told you what to do."

"I know it. Thank you."

Go back the next day. "Doctor, I am sick."

"I gave you the diagnosis two days ago and the solution."

"I know it."

You do the same the third day, fourth day, and fifth day. Everyday you keep going back, you keep getting the same diagnosis.

Our ministers have spent months with people – every session, same diagnosis, same illness. What is the solution? Get free. "I do not want to be free." "Why are you showing up here then?" "I need help." "I am trying to help you." "I know it, thank you." Spiritual roots must be identified and revealed by the person, by the Holy Spirit, by the Word, by someone God has set in place with discernment. One of the nine gifts of the Holy Spirit in 1 Corinthians 12 is discerning of spirits. Every believer should be able to discern spirits.

Deal With It

Secondly, the root must not only be identified and revealed, but it must be dealt with decisively and quickly.

"Well, thank you Pastor for your diagnosis. Maybe I will call you next year."

"Well, thank you Pastor, I will pray about it."

You need deliverance; you need to deal with this in your life.

Look at any tree out there. The big root was not always big. One day it was little and it grew up. There was a time when your spiritual problems were little. Then they grew up on you and overtook you like a wild vine.

After identification in revelation, that root must be dealt with decisively and quickly.

Resist it!

Thirdly, steps must be taken to prevent re-growth.

How would you prevent re-growth of Bitterness? If you really want to be spiritual about this, when wrong is done to you, you do not pay attention to it because you understand so clearly that you do not have to be affected by it.

When you look at a tree you can sometimes tell what kind of tree it is; oak, elm, pine. It has bark and leaves, a trunk and limbs. That is the fruit of the root. It is not only the fruit of the root. It is the fruit of the seed of the root. The root does not exist just by itself; it comes from a seed. The tree, including the trunk from the ground on up, is the outward manifestation.

I can stand here and preach to you. I can give you understanding. I can preach and I can teach and I can blister your ears with truth, just like a fire would hit that tree and it would burn all the leaves and all the bad fruit off. For a few days you would walk around spiritually naked without the obvious result of the fruit of that root. But the root still has not been dealt with. Many people I deal with are convicted. For a season, it looks like they are free. But the old problem comes back again and we have to deal with it all over again.

Why? Because the root was not dealt with. I can preach the devil right out of you but I might not be able to keep him away from you, if you like him. I may preach your devils off you, but they can grow back because they are still nourished by the roots.

Remember when King David came around Saul when he was insane. The evil spirit of insanity was all over King Saul. David would come and play the music of God. The evil spirit could not handle it and would depart. But when David walked away, and the music of God walked away, the evil spirit came back because Saul loved David's music, but he did not love God.

Your freedom will not come without your relationship with God being established. You may want to be free of the bad fruit, but you are not going to be free of it unless you get the seed of hell out of you.

Eliminate the Seed

What are the steps to get rid of the seed of hell within? The first step is teaching, giving an understanding, and bringing the problem into focus. It is an x-ray vision of spiritual things. If we cut the tree down, we still have the stump, and it is obvious. Recognizing and observing Bitterness or family separation in our lives or the lives of others is also obvious.

Because you recognize your problem or your family tree's problem – that is not a solution. Discernment by itself is not freedom. You can discern the fruit on the tree, you can discern the tree and you can know everything about yourself spiritually. You could write a book about your evil tree, but it does not mean you are free. To teach does not produce freedom. To know the truth, the truth shall make you free. But there has to be an application. You have to participate in wanting to be a different kind of tree.

When a tree is cut down, the stump remains and the root system remains. Let me give you an example. We might be after rejection, and we may see the fruit of rejection. Some of the fruits of Rejection are adultery, fornication, fantasy lust – these are leaves. These are manifestations of the root. But the root behind the scenes is Rejection. You may fall out of agreement with adultery and fornication and any other area. But if you have not dealt with the Rejection, you are not going to have very good success with the fruit. They are going to grow right back again.

All people who get into addictions, pornography, various types of sexual behavior that are not permitted by God, and all adultery, fornication, masturbation, all inordinate sexual activity, and inordinate affection - all are rooted in a need to be loved. The need to be loved is fueled by Rejection. You cannot solve any of the manifestations of what I have just said if you do not deal with Rejection. The need to be loved is the driving force.

Adultery, fornication, and fantasy are leaves – the symptoms. But the root is Rejection and an Unloving spirit. Roots do not exist alone but are tangled together in a supply and dependency mode, feeding into each other big and small. That is why sometimes when it comes to ministry and getting your lives straightened out, we walk into a tangled mess.

We might be dealing with Rejection today, but there are probably 150 other areas that need to be dealt with also. They all link together; they are all forming together. Unless you bind the strong man, you cannot spoil his house. You are never going to be healed unless you deal with Bitterness. You must walk in forgiveness because God has said in His Word in Matthew 18 that He is just not going to compromise what is best for you.

We are laying a foundation for freedom. Your problems are not little individual jars sitting on a shelf that we just take one jar off at a time and dump out the contents. I wish it were that easy. We could do deliverance on jar number one, jar number two, jar number three, until we reach number 48. We just dump the contents out and deal with it. But there is no order because we are a product of dozens and dozens of generations of separation from God in our family trees, and it is a tangled mess spiritually.

You need deliverance if you cannot be free, no matter how much you try to get before God. That is an indication that you need deliverance. There is a power that is greater than your will and greater than your intent. This is where deliverance is so very important in the Christian church.

Sometimes deliverance is not necessary for every person. Sometimes people are changed and made free, and there is no direct deliverance.

If a person is not delivered, it is an indication something has a right to that person's life that has not been dealt with, based on the scripture, "The curse causeless does not come."

As the bird by wandering, as the swallow by flying, so the curse causeless shall not come.   Proverbs 26:2

Your life can be a tangled system of roots. Pulling up the roots is a life-changing experience. Digging up the roots is a life-changing experience.

Being free from Rejection is a life changing experience! Amen.